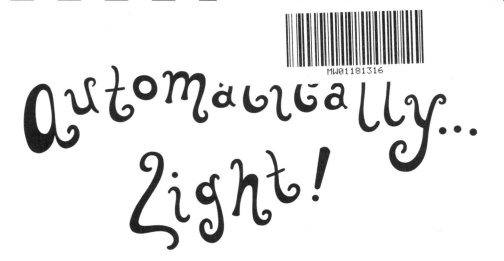

automatically... Light!

Easy Low-Fat Recipes Using Time-Saving Appliances And The Heatproof Oven Bag

by Pat Leontsinis

AUTOCOOK L.L.C., St. Louis, Missouri

First Printing 1997

Printed in the United States of America by The Wimmer Companies, Inc., Memphis, TN

Designed by Parallel Design Inc., St. Louis, MO

Nutrition Consultants:
Patricia A. Ebsworth, B.A., B.S., Foods and Nutrition
Suzanne R. Switzer, M.S., R.D.

Library of Congress Catalog Card Number: 97-93565
ISBN: 0-9658382-7-7

Printed in the USA by
WIMMER
The Wimmer Companies
Memphis

parallel design inc.

To my parents, Chris and Mary,
who instilled in me a love of
innovation in all things

Acknowledgments

My family played an enormous role in the development of this book and I would like to thank George, Anne and Michelle for all of their help with the creation and endless tasting of recipes. Sharon Roberson provided many hours of typing. Paul Edwards never wavered in his support for my concept. Finally, my sincere appreciation is extended to Parallel Design Inc. and especially to Mary Jo Evertowski for bringing my ideas and concepts to fruition.

Notice: The information in Automatically...Light! is intended to help you prepare tasty, healthy, low-fat recipes using certain appliances and the heatproof oven bag. This book should be used as a guide and not as the ultimate source of information regarding these appliances and the oven bag. Always consult the directions which accompanied your appliance or heatproof oven bags before preparing the recipe. Accordingly, the author and AUTOCOOK, L.L.C. shall have neither liability nor responsibility to any person or entity with respect to any loss or damage caused, or alleged to be caused, directly or indirectly, by the information concerning appliances or heatproof oven bags contained in this book. **If you do not wish to be bound by the above, you may return this book to the publisher for a full refund.**

Table of Contents

What "Automatically... Light!" is All About

I'm a lazy cook. No, make that, I'm a lazy cook who wants to eat tasty, healthy, home-cooked foods. What to do? Over the years, I've created recipes for my family which use certain time-saving appliances (the microwave, slow cooker, ice cream machine, rice cooker, automatic bread machine and grill) and the much neglected heatproof oven bag. When we began to observe the "eat less than 30% of Calories from fat" guideline as out-lined by the American Heart Association, the American Cancer Society, the National Center for Nutrition and Dietetics, The American Diabetes Association and the Surgeon General of the U.S. (whew!), I was astonished to discover almost no cookbooks for appli-ances which observe this "rule". It was then that I began to develop recipes that fit this guideline for these appliances and the heatproof oven bag. Some save preparation time, some save cooking time, some save cleanup time and some (one might say the best) combine all of these savings. After encouragement from friends and family, I'm sharing these recipes with you in "Automatically... Light!". Make no mistake, this is not a gourmet cookbook. Far from it. It's a cookbook for busy people. While recipes in this cookbook do not guarantee complete nutrition, busy people can use them to prepare with little effort nutritious and relatively low-fat meals. Most recipes can literally be prepared by combining all ingredients at one time and then walking away, no basting, no watching, no turning. The degree of "automatic cooking" will depend on the appliance, but in every case, less attention will be required than a standard stove-top or oven recipe.

Specific appliances produce better results than others with certain types of foods. For example: say "slow cooker", we think soups; say "vegetables", we think microwave. And generally, these assumptions are accurate. Cookbooks for appliances are usually written for the use of a single appliance and frequently, merely to make the cookbook more "complete", will include recipes that are not well suited for that particular appliance. What is really unique about this cookbook is that it contains a combination of my favorite tried and true low-fat recipes adapted for use in **several** time-saving appliances and the heatproof oven bag. I have concentrated on the best use of each type of appliance and cooking technique for low-fat recipes. The **techniques** of low-fat cooking incorporated in the recipes are as important as the recipes themselves. And, of course, you too can modify your favorite recipes by following this approach to cooking!

You may not own all of the appliances featured in this cookbook. An alter-native technique using the oven or cooktop is included for each recipe. The

result will generally be the same, but with more cooking attention and/or cleanup time and effort. References to instructions common to both the primary and the alternate recipe are made by the use of "*" 's.

Menus are included which utilize the appliances and the heatproof oven bag to create "automatic" meals. As with most things, the key to success is a little advance planning. I have listed on page 257 pantry-ready foods to keep on hand which will enable you to easily prepare these recipes, thus encouraging healthy eating. Most, if not all, may be found at your local supermarket.

A computer program, Nutritionist IV, was used to compute the caloric and nutritional breakdown for the recipes and menus using a database derived from several important nutrient content resources, including the U.S. Department of Agriculture (USDA) Agricultural Handbook #8, Vol. 1-21 and supplements, 1977-1992. Each recipe includes the following nutrient analysis: Calories, protein, carbohydrate, fat, fiber, cholesterol and sodium as well as percentage of fat per serving. This analysis refers to the **primary recipe** which is in the majority of cases identical to the analysis of the alternate. When a recipe was especially high in a nutrient, I noted this in the introduction on the recipe page. For example, a recipe high in beta carotene was expressed in R.E. Units, a term for Retinol Equivalents which includes both beta carotene in plants and retinol in animal source foods. On very few occasions, when a food item was not listed in the program, data was obtained from the manufacturer's food label.

Now, let's get **"Automatically...Light!"**

A Little Serious Talk
About Low-Fat Diets

This is a cookbook consisting of time-saving recipes and low-fat cooking techniques (using certain appliances and the heatproof oven bag) which can help to achieve a low-fat diet. Guidelines from recognized health authorities such as the American Heart Association and the American Cancer Society suggest that a low-fat diet can help prevent heart disease and cancer. These and other noted organizations such as the American Dietetic Association advise the public to reduce their percentage of fat Calories to 30% or less of their total Calories. Emphasis is also on the balance of the various types of dietary fat: 10% of daily Calories should come from saturated fat, 10% from monounsaturated fat and 10% from polyunsaturated fat. In addition, it has been suggested that 4% of the daily fat Calories should include essential fatty acids, a type of polyunsaturated fat. Since saturated fat has been revealed in numerous studies to be the greatest dietary offender in heart disease promotion, I have attempted to maintain the 30% total fat and 10% saturated fat Calories ratio in the included recipes. Keep in mind that it is not the fat content of just one meal but the total fat for the day and even several days that "counts". Some cookbooks produce the caloric and nutritional breakdown for a combination of meat **and** vegetable accompaniment, (beef and pasta, pork and rice), in order to lower the fat percentage of the meat. Recipes in this cookbook indicate the nutritional breakdown for the meat alone. As a result, some may be slightly greater than 30% fat content, but I'll suggest ways to lower this percentage by adding low-fat vegetable accompaniments. At times, the fat percentage of individual foods can be misleading. (A salad dressing which is low in Calories may have a high fat percentage.) In these cases, look at the actual fat grams which should be around 2 grams or less per serving.

I have incorporated the guidelines discussed above in my recipes by selecting oils that meet these recommendations. Whenever a recipe calls for added fat, I suggest using liquid plant oils such as canola, soybean, corn oil or sunflower oil; or, where noted, use olive oil. All fat in food, whether solid or liquid, is 100% fat and has 9 Calories per gram. However each fat is unique in its make-up. Generally, animal sources of fat (solid fats such as butter) are high in saturated fat and cholesterol. (Note that cholesterol intake should be limited to less than 300 mg per day.) Fish fat is high in polyunsaturated omega-3-fatty acids. Studies have shown that omega-3-fatty acids, essential fats, help prevent both heart disease and certain cancers. In addition to fish, canola and soybean oils are good sources of omega-3-fatty acids. On the other hand, plant fats (liquid oils) are high in other unsaturated fatty acids and have no cholesterol. (Exceptions are the tropical plant oils: coconut, palm and palm kernel oil, which are high in saturated fat.) Olive oil is high in oleic acid, a monounsaturated fatty acid, and has no cholesterol.

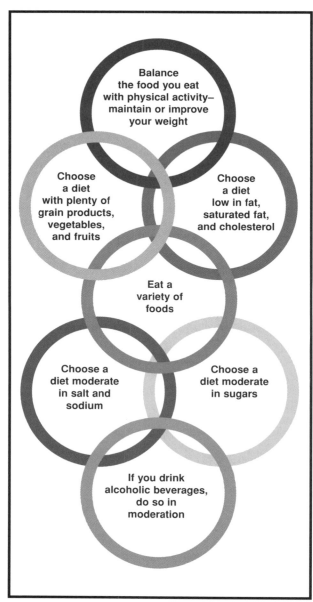

Figure 1: Dietary Guidelines for Americans
Fourth Edition, 1995
U.S. Department of Agriculture
U.S. Department of Health and Human Services

Diets high in this monounsaturated fatty acid such as those consumed in countries along the Mediterranean Sea have been observed to be protective against heart disease and certain cancers. Research has demonstrated that consumption of hardened oils (hydrogenated) can promote an elevation of blood cholesterol similar to the consumption of saturated fat.

Nutritionists have long known that a well balanced diet is the cornerstone to good health and that following the suggestions put forth in the United States Department of Agriculture (USDA) and the Department of Health and Human Services (DHHS) "Dietary Guidelines For Americans" will help achieve this goal. *(See Figure 1)* Two of these guidelines refer to proper weight and the fat content of the diet. The 10th edition of the Recommended Dietary Allowances (RDA), 1989, contains the following chart, *(See Figure 2, page 5)* which contains median height and weight and corresponding recommended energy intake. Use of a table such as this is one of many ways of estimating what an individual's healthy weight should be and the approximate caloric intake needed to maintain that weight. Large or multiple portions and therefore excessive caloric intake will defeat the benefits of a low-fat balanced diet. Once you have established your approximate Calorie level to

Age	Weight		Height		Average Energy Allowance			
(yr)	kg	lb	cm	in	REE[a] (kcal/day)	Multiples of REE[b]	kcal/kg	kcal/day[c]
Infants								
0.0-0.5	6	13	60	24	320		108	650
0.5-1.0	9	20	71	28	500		98	850
Children								
1-3	13	29	90	35	740		102	1300
4-6	20	44	112	44	950		90	1800
7-10	28	62	132	52	1130		70	2000
Males								
11-14	45	99	157	62	1440	1.70	55	2500
15-18	66	145	176	69	1760	1.67	45	3000
19-24	72	160	177	70	1780	1.67	40	2900
25-50	79	174	176	70	1800	1.60	37	2900
51+	77	170	173	68	1530	1.50	30	2300
Females								
11-14	46	101	157	62	1310	1.67	47	2200
15-18	55	120	163	64	1370	1.60	40	2200
19-24	58	128	164	65	1350	1.60	38	2200
25-50	63	138	163	64	1380	1.55	36	2200
51+	65	143	160	63	1280	1.50	30	1900
Pregnant (2nd and 3rd trimesters)								+300
Lactating								+500

a REE (resting energy expenditure) represents the energy expended by a person at rest under normal conditions.

b Recommended energy allowances assume light-to-moderate activity and were calculated by multiplying the REE by an activity factor

c Average energy allowances have been rounded

Source: Recommended Dietary Allowances, ©1989 by the National Academy of Sciences, National Academy Press, Washington, D.C.

*Figure 2: **Median Heights and Weights and Recommended Energy Intakes (United States)***

(The terms kcal and Calorie are used interchangeably.)

To determine the number of fat grams for your daily caloric intake:
Using the HEIGHT AND WEIGHT Chart in Figure 2, assume the Calories for an active 25 year old female. Multiply 2200 Calories by 30% = 660 Calories a day can come from fat. Divide this number by 9 (fat contains 9 Calories per gram) which results in 53 grams - the number of grams of fat the person in this example could eat daily and remain under the 30% guideline.

Energy released from energy-yielding nutrients in food are measured in Calories. Carbohydrates and protein contain 4 Calories per gram and, as noted above, fat contains 9 Calories per gram. To calculate the total Calories and the percentage of Calories derived from fat for a food, a series of simple calculations can be performed, shown below using an 8 ounce bowl of chicken noodle soup which contains 11 grams of carbohydrate, 11 grams of protein and 3 grams of fat as an example:

11 g carbohydrate	x	4 Calories/g = 44 Calories
11 g protein	x	4 Calories/g = 44 Calories
3 g fat	x	9 Calories/g = 27 Calories
		Total = 115 Calories

The percentage of Calories each of the energy nutrients contributes to the total can be calculated by dividing the nutrient Calories by the total number of Calories.
To determine the percentage of Calories from fat:
27 divided by 115 = 0.2348 (rounded to 0.23)
To get the percentage, multiply by 100:
0.23 x 100 = 23%
This bowl of chicken noodle soup contains **23% fat**.

Figure 3

maintain a healthy weight, then you are ready to calculate daily alloted grams of fat at 30% of total Calories. *(See Figure 3)* Oh, come on, ...it's easy!

To assist people in their selection of a healthy diet, the USDA created the "Food Guide Pyramid". *(See Figure 4, page7)* This acts as a visual aid in teaching us the recommended serving selections from each food group that will provide the nutrients so necessary for good health. Remember to include all food groups to achieve balance and moderation. Should servings from a food group fall below the recommended number or be completely lacking, those contributing nutrients must be made up by other means. For example, vegetarians who eat only plant source foods need to replace the levels of those nutrients which would have been provided by animal source foods.

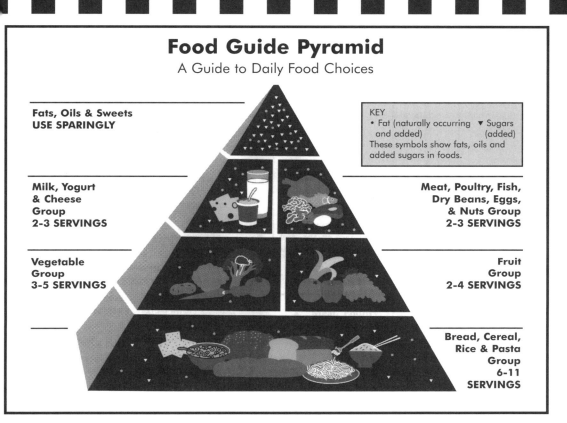

Food Guide Pyramid
A Guide to Daily Food Choices

Fats, Oils & Sweets
USE SPARINGLY

KEY
• Fat (naturally occurring   ▼ Sugars
  and added)   (added)
These symbols show fats, oils and
added sugars in foods.

Milk, Yogurt
& Cheese
Group
2-3 SERVINGS

Meat, Poultry, Fish,
Dry Beans, Eggs,
& Nuts Group
2-3 SERVINGS

Vegetable
Group
3-5 SERVINGS

Fruit
Group
2-4 SERVINGS

Bread, Cereal,
Rice & Pasta
Group
6-11
SERVINGS

Figure 4: ***Food Guide Pyramid***
U.S. Department of Agriculture, U.S. Department of Health and Human Services

The Mediterranean influence in some of the recipes is a result of my Greek heritage. That part of the world has always enjoyed a diet high in fruits, vegetables, grains and beans. Red meat was considered a delicacy and was served very infrequently as were sweets. They used olive oil, a monounsaturated fat, almost exclusively. One might say they have always been into healthy food choices.

Since nutrition is the cornerstone, but not the only stone, which builds good health, we must include routine exercise and stress reduction as part of our total health plan. So to help give you more time for yourself, I have created "Automatically...Light!".

Miscellaneous Tips and Tidbits

The new 1995 USDA Dietary Guidelines For Americans suggest that Americans choose a diet moderate in sodium (eg. table salt). As I tested and developed the included recipes, I added salt to my own taste. However, you can always add less or no salt or perhaps more salt to suit your own taste. Each recipe is accompanied by its own nutrient analysis which includes the sodium content. It is helpful to read labels for sodium content when choosing ingredients for recipes as sodium content can vary greatly among different brands of the same type of product. Some packaged foods lend themselves to "rinsing" away sodium. Take the time to read labels; you will become a more knowledgeable consumer!

The Dietary Guidelines also advise us to choose plenty of vegetables. Don't hesitate to use frozen vegetables, especially those with no added salt. They are generally frozen immediately after harvest and are considered nutritionally equal to the fresh vegetables in the supermarket.

I have repeated many sauces used with meat and vegetables in their own section in order to indicate sauce nutrients, alone. Use these on other meats and vegetables of your choice.

A little talk about meat. Beef graded "good" turns out to be doubly good for us low-fat eaters. First, it's cheaper than choice or prime. Second, it's lower in fat. It doesn't have the "marbling" of fat throughout which the more expensive cuts contain. This results in a somewhat tougher piece of meat which is irrelevant when braising but more important when roasting or grilling. Marinating the meat will break down the connective tissue. By the way, for a wonderful meat taste which is very low in Calories, fat and cholesterol compared to beef, chicken, and turkey, you must try bison. I feel it can be successfully substituted in most of the included beef recipes. Look for it at your local supermarket. Also, be alert when purchasing ground turkey! Some commercial packaged ground turkey contains not only a mixture of light and dark meat, but may also include the skin. This results in a fat content over 50%. When only the breast is used, the fat percentage drops to under 10%. All recipes used here assume the use of ground turkey breast only, generally only sold fresh, not frozen. Please try to avoid eating poultry skin, and if you can't bear to cook poultry skinless, skim the resulting broth to remove all fat before using the broth for gravies and sauces.

I couldn't get along without three wonderful gadgets. A food scale is indispensible, especially when using the microwave which can be very fussy where weight and time are closely tied to success. The instant-read thermometer is also necessary for both the microwave and the grill and for appliances which will not allow the thermometer to be inserted in the meat throughout the cooking process. And finally, I recommend the gravy skimmer which allows fat to be skimmed by a spout which sits at the top of the cup. (Another method to skim fat is to pour the broth into a heavy-duty zip-top bag, seal it, place it in a bowl and let it sit for a few minutes so the fat will rise. Then cut one bottom corner of the bag and let the broth drain until the fat reaches the bottom. Then quickly remove the bag from the bowl.)

When a recipe calls for "defatted" broth, either use purchased fat-free broth or chill an unopened can of the standard variety for at least one hour. Open the chilled can and immediately remove accumulated fat from the top.

There are many recipes which include alcohol either in the marinade or the actual cooking. Substitute an acidic liquid such as lemon juice in the marinade and a meat or vegetable broth during the cooking, if desired. Alcohol contains 7 Calories per gram and will only be indicated if there is greater than 1% calories from alcohol in the recipe. Most alcohol "burns off" and leaves only the flavor, thus decreasing the Calories.

Additional tips are included with the recipes. All of the tips can be incorporated into a daily routine of low-fat eating.

The Appliances, The Heatproof Oven Bag, and "Automatic" Low-Fat Cooking

Always refer to the manufacturer's instructions which accompanied your appliance when using that appliance. It would be impossible to produce recipes to take into account every idiosyncrasy which each appliance may have. Therefore, these recipes should be used as guidelines which can and should be modified, whenever necessary, to fit your own appliance.

 THE MICROWAVE is probably the least **well**-used appliance in the kitchen. Used mainly for reheating foods, I'm surprised that so little cooking is done in this handiest of all machines. Much has to do with fear of the microwave and its finicky nature (yes, it's very easy to produce a rubbery chicken breast). But I believe a great deal has to do with inertia. It takes a little reading, time and practice to "get it right." Maybe the motivation of low-fat results will be all that you need to take advantage of this marvelous appliance!

If you want to know **how** a microwave works, please read your appliance manual. What you need to know for low-fat cooking in the microwave is that **fats are generally not needed** since in the microwave, food cooks in its own juices and does not require a fat to prevent sticking. **Foods cook quickly, so more nutrients and flavor are retained. This minimizes the need for additional fats**, which, as we all know too well, add flavor to foods. It's also so nice to be able to cook in and serve from the same dish (not a pot or a pan), and then clean it in the dishwasher.

A few tips. The microwave cooks from the outside in, so it's preferable to place foods in a ring along the outside of the dish, stir halfway through to disperse food, or use a "doughnut" shaped dish (or place an inverted, microwave-safe glass in the center of the dish to get a doughnut shape effect). Evenly shaped foods cook best, and they cook the very best in a round container. Foods cooked in the microwave continue to cook even after they've been removed. Test for doneness after the resting time specified in the recipe. To determine whether a dish is microwave-safe, fill a 2-cup measure with 1 cup cold water, and place it in the oven next to the dish to be tested. Heat 1 minute at high temperature. If the water is hot and the dish is cool, the dish is microwave-safe. If the dish is hot, it is probably not safe.

Included microwave recipes have been tested in a 650 watt microwave. If you're using a

900 watt microwave, reduce power 10% from that specified in the recipe; for 1000 watts, reduce power 20%. I don't recommend cooking in a microwave lower than 600 watts of power, but if you'd like to try it, increase the cooking time slightly and test the food periodically. (To test your microwave for wattage, fill a 2-cup measure with 1 cup cold water. Microwave at high power until the water starts to boil. If it boils in 3 minutes or less, it is a "high power oven" over 600 watts.)

Best uses: The microwave produces the best results on foods conventionally cooked by moist heat such as vegetables, fruits, and sauces, and also on protein rich foods, such as fish and poultry (in relatively small quantities). It's also great for quick cooking. How else could you "bake" a two-pound meatloaf in 25 minutes?

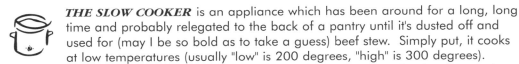

THE SLOW COOKER is an appliance which has been around for a long, long time and probably relegated to the back of a pantry until it's dusted off and used for (may I be so bold as to take a guess) beef stew. Simply put, it cooks at low temperatures (usually "low" is 200 degrees, "high" is 300 degrees). When liquid is added to food, it produces a slow moist environment for the slow cooker which is the optimum way to tenderize meat. How does this process benefit low-fat cooking? **Lean low-fat meats tend to be tough and have a relatively high content of connective tissue. Slow moist heat softens connective tissue and thereby tenderizes the meat.** (And nutrients are not cooked away, either.) Basically, this is braising or stewing. Generally, braising requires the browning of meat before liquid is added; but due to the very low heat used in the slow cooker, it is not necessary, since the juices will not be cooked out of the meat. Dried beans are a wonderful source of complex carbohydrates which are so crucial to a well-balanced diet; but who has time to stand over a pot of bean soup for hours? Use the slow cooker. There's no better appliance for cooking beans. In fact, it's wonderful for just about any soup. This appliance **is** "automatic" cooking since you can turn it on and walk away for a long time, 8 hours or even 24 hours. Due to its very low heat output, it is considered one of the few appliances safe to leave on when you're not at home. It's also helpful for busy families who can't seem to eat on the same schedule as it keeps food warm and looks good at the same time.

Best uses: The slow cooker has never seen a tough cut of meat it can't tenderize. Beans, soups and sauces are always tasty. Assemble the dish the night before, plug it in the next morning and then bye-bye till dinner.

THE ICE CREAM MACHINE is such a delightful appliance. **When you're making a frozen dessert using fruit, whether fresh, frozen, or canned, there's no guilt, since you know you're going to give your family and/or friends a sweet which is both healthful and low-fat.**

And it just couldn't be easier. Prepare the fruit mix in advance (even a couple of days in advance), keep it refrigerated, and freeze it at the last minute if you choose. Or freeze it in advance and store it until it's time to serve. Since there is now such a variety of these machines, ranging from the very reasonable (store the insulated bowl in the freezer so it's always ready) to the very expensive (ready anytime, just plug in). Basically, when I discuss this "automatic" appliance, I'm not referring to the old-fashioned "ice cubes, salt, and hand-crank" model. But there's no reason the included recipes won't work in that model. It's just not easy. I also did not feel there was a need to include a great variety of recipes for this machine since it's so easy to substitute one type of fruit and flavoring for the basic recipes.

Best uses: Sorbet, sherbet, frozen yogurt. Freeze your favorite fruit frequently.
(Isn't this fun?)

 THE RICE COOKER is just for cooking rice. Wrong. It's a wonderful all-around appliance useful for any food cooked or steamed in a pot on the stovetop. The time-saving benefit is that after you turn it on, you walk away. **No standing around for the liquid to boil so that you can reduce heat to a simmer. It's "automatic".** Typically, the machine turns itself off when the water has been completely absorbed, but I suggest in most recipes that you set a timer and return at a specified time to turn it off or unplug it yourself. This prevents overdrying of foods which can sometimes happen. Low-fat cooking is a breeze since most pots are nonstick. Spray anyway with nonstick cooking spray to aid in effortless cleanup. In addition to your own collection of home appliances, the rice cooker can be a boon to the student in a dorm, a homeowner in the midst of remodeling, or in any situation where the kitchen facilities are limited or where an additional burner is needed. And it's so handy to serve from the cooking pot. (Included recipes which utilize the rice cooker assume the use of the common variety which consists of a pan which fits in a container with a heating element in the base. There is no water reservoir in this model. A steaming pan, basket, rack, or plate is usually included.) I have included a timing chart for cooking a few varieties of rice and grains using a 1 1/2-quart model. I encourage you to make your own notes on this chart with cooking times for your machine. It's very helpful to know how much time the food will take to cook so you can set a timer and "walk away". Experiment with the "keep warm" feature, as some models work better than others. As stated earlier, the easiest way to assure a moist result is to turn off and/or unplug the machine when cooking has completed. When modifying your own recipes for the rice cooker, keep in mind that some models will require the addition of slightly more liquid due to increased moisture loss.

Best uses: Rice dishes, grain dishes, steamed fish, shellfish and steamed desserts. Turn it on; then walk away.

THE AUTOMATIC BREAD MACHINE is an appliance with a "love - hate" problem. Some people love it (I've worn out two machines in 4 years), some people hate it. They probably hate it because they bought it and don't use it. I believe that much ambivalence is related to the timer (an important feature) and whether you're willing to use it or not. There's nothing better than warm bread for breakfast but you must be willing to let that little machine start its work in the middle of the night. Or second best, to walk into your home after a long day to the aroma of bread baking for dinner. (The machine will start early in the afternoon.) In both cases, you prepare the ingredients (5 minutes, maximum), set the timer and leave. **This is "automatic" and probably the most time-saving appliance around.** Very few of us will take the time to bake bread regularly using the manual method since it requires our being around most of the day. **And, of course, since you select the ingredients, low-fat baking is a snap.** The adage that you mustn't eat bread because it's fattening is just old-fashioned and wrong. As we saw earlier in the food pyramid on page 7, the "bread, cereal, rice and pasta group" should provide the **most** daily measured servings. Because you choose the ingredients, they can be whatever you want: the most nutritious, high fiber, low calorie, low-fat and, of course, preservative-free. Other features which your machine may have are: "Dough only" setting mixes the ingredients and allows the dough to rise once and you must then remove the dough, complete the recipe and bake the bread manually; "Sweet bread or cake" setting combines the ingredients and bakes it with no additional mix or rise cycles; "Jam" setting boils for about 1 hour. These are all splendid features and can be very useful. If your machine does not have them, use the alternate recipe which I've provided.

Best uses: All kinds of breads as well as jams and cakes if your machine provides these features.

THE GRILL is a generic term for any of a number of gadgets, appliances and kettles all of which have one thing in common: they all facilitate the cooking of food directly over or under a source of heat. Therefore, the broiler may be included in this group. However, I've found that cooking over the heat source produces better results than under the heat source. (Broiling requires careful attention to prevent burning and I also greatly dislike cleaning the broiler pan and oven.) I like the result which the hot grate directly touching the food produces. **Grilling is one of the healthiest ways to cook meat, since most of the fat drains away and results in literally fat-free cooking of the meat.** Grilling allows for retention of moisture and flavor of the food since the heat sears the outside quickly. **"Automatic cooking"** when applied to grilling does not refer to the charcoal kettle, but to the gas or electric grill, found either indoors (as part of the stovetop) or outdoors, or one of the myriad of grill "appliances" which can be purchased. Automatic, in these cases, refers to the speed of cooking, the walk-away aspect, the easy preheating and the minimal cleanup. It's much easier to leave a piece of meat on a covered grill and come back to turn it, than it is to saute the same cut of meat on the stovetop. And there's no messy pan to wash. Many of these indoor appliances have a lid which prevents the nuisance of smoke and grease in the kitchen, while some have a thermostat to control the heat, and others are simply ridged pans which can be used either under the broiler or on the stovetop (the ridges help to drain the fat). A particular favorite of mine is a gadget which is the combination of a water reservoir which sits around the heat source on the stovetop and a domed, ridged, nonstick grill which sits on top of the reservoir. Fat drains through holes in the grill into the water which eliminates smoke and odors. Keep in mind that the above mentioned grills may require a variety of cooking times. Alter cooking times accordingly. All recipes were tested on a standard gas grill, indoor electric grill or electric broiler. At times a grill rack - a tray with small holes which sits on the grate - will be required for cooking delicate fish, vegetables or fruit. Always spray the rack and/or grate before heating with nonstick vegetable spray.

Best uses: Tender cuts of meat, marinated meat, vegetables and fruit.

THE HEATPROOF OVEN BAG is a very inexpensive kitchen aid which has been neglected. It is made from either a nylon or polyester plastic material which is safe to use in the oven at a wide range of temperatures, generally not to exceed 400 degrees. **Do not confuse the heatproof oven bag with the plastic food storage bag which is not heatproof!** The heatproof oven bag provides, by far, the most automatic method to roast meat, chicken and vegetables. The food "bastes itself" with moisture retained in the bag as it browns, a feature which also makes this a most desirable product for low-fat cooking as virtually no additional fat is required. Juices can't escape, yet the clear nature of the heatproof oven bag allows the heat to penetrate and brown the food. Smaller quantities of fat are necessary in food preparation with the heatproof oven bag as the bag does not allow the fat to stick to the pan, instead small amounts adhere to the food and add flavor. The heatproof oven bag's many other advantages include: (1) it's possible to marinate food and cook in the same heatproof oven bag; (2) microwaving is a joy as moisture and flavor are retained; (3) unlike many other types of plastic, direct food contact with this product, while cooking, is FDA (Food & Drug Administration) approved; (4) flavor and odor transfer between foods sharing an oven is minimized; (5) meat cooking times may be shortened while shrinkage is reduced; (6) food is generally moister along with decreased loss of vitamins and minerals; (7) it's possible to cook, freeze the contents and then reheat, all in the same heatproof oven bag; (8) most heatproof oven bags are Kosher approved; (9) there's never a messy pan to wash. I must confess, lazy me, I sometimes slit the bag and serve from it, saving myself the trouble of washing a serving plate. Try the no-mess, no-cleanup technique for boiling pasta in the heatproof oven bag in the microwave on page 232.

Special notes: All recipes were tested in 14x17-inch or 14x20-inch oven bags. Follow the instructions which accompany the oven bag when preparing the bag for use. To insert food into the bag easily, make a "cuff" at the opening by folding back the end. The heatproof oven bag should **always** be placed in a baking pan or dish. Always pre-heat the oven before using the heatproof oven bag. Recipes will sometimes specify a lower temperature with some meats than is usual due to the special efficiency of the heatproof oven bag. Since heatproof oven bag manufacturers use different types of materials for their bags, cooking times may vary. Always use a meat thermometer, inserted through the bag, and increase cooking times, if necessary. Manufacturer's oven bag directions vary regarding the addition of flour. (When roasting meats or preparing recipes which contain a fairly large amount of liquid, flour should always be added.) Some do not require flour, while others require a fixed amount (to prevent bump boiling and bursting). If a recipe in this cookbook utilizes a heatproof oven bag and does not specify flour and you choose to use an oven bag which requires flour, prepare the recipe as directed and choose one of the following options: (1) shake the directed amount of flour in the oven bag and allow the flour which does not adhere to the bag to settle in one corner; or (2) if the addition of flour does not seem appropriate for the recipe, keep the heatproof oven bag **open**, vent the bag as directed on the package, and "cuff" the open end so the excess does not extend outside the pan or dish. If you choose option (2), the bag will not be used as an oven bag but merely as a heatproof plastic covering. (Recipe results may be slightly different.) This option (2) technique will not be appropriate for cooking in the microwave as microwave-cooking generally requires food to be tightly covered.

Best uses: Where do I start? Turkey, chicken, beef, pork, lamb, vegetables, fruit and pasta.

Starts and Snacks

Starts and Snacks

Notes

Layered Tuna and Roasted Red Pepper Spread

A contrast in colors and flavors, quick and healthy.

1/4 cup low-fat cottage cheese
1 (6 1/2-ounce) can tuna, packed in water, drained
3 tablespoons fat-free mayonnaise
3 tablespoons ripe olives, sliced
3 tablespoons green onions, minced, including the tender green part
1 slice white bread, torn into large pieces
3/4 teaspoon lemon juice
1 garlic clove
1/2 teaspoon dried basil leaves
1/2 teaspoon salt
1/8 teaspoon white pepper

Place cottage cheese in a small sieve and rinse with water. Drain well. Puree with remaining ingredients through white pepper in a food processor. (Or puree in small batches in a blender.) Spread on a 10-inch **microwave**-safe plate.

15 sun dried tomatoes (not oil packed), about 1/2 cup
1 (7-ounce) jar roasted red peppers, drained
1 (4 1/2-ounce) can chopped mild green chilies, drained
1/2 teaspoon ground cumin

Soak tomatoes in hot water for about 5 minutes, or until softened and water has become rosy. Drain. Puree tomatoes through cumin in a food processor. Carefully drop large spoonsful of pepper mixture on tuna, then spread with a spatula. Cook in the microwave on medium-high (50%) for 5 minutes or until warmed through. (Rotate plate 1/2 turn halfway through cooking time if microwave does not have a carousel.)

Serve warm with thin slices of diagonally cut French bread or low-fat crackers.

10% calories from fat per serving

Yield: 16 (2-tablespoon) servings
Nutrient content per serving:
Calories: 36   Fat: 0.4 g   Protein: 3.6 g   Carbohydrate: 4.4 g
Sodium: 223 mg   Cholesterol: 3.3 mg   Fiber: 0.5 g

Alternate Method: Layer tuna and pepper mixtures in a heatproof plate. Bake in a 350 degree oven until warmed through, about 20 minutes.

Spinach Feta Squares With Salsa

If you're lucky enough to have a "cake" cycle on your bread machine, this technique will save both mixing bowls and a baking pan; otherwise just use the alternate method.

1 cup onion, chopped
1/4 cup chicken broth

Place onion and broth in a **microwave**-safe bowl. Cover. Cook on high for 3 minutes or until onion is soft.

4 (10-ounce) packages frozen chopped spinach, thawed and squeezed dry in a tea towel or paper towels
2 eggs
2 egg whites

Combine onion, broth, spinach and eggs in a food processor. Puree. (Or puree small batches in a blender.) Turn into the bread machine pan which has been lightly sprayed with nonstick cooking spray.

1/2 cup fat-free Parmesan cheese, grated
1/4 cup Yogurt Cheese (page 235) or fat-free sour cream
2 garlic cloves, minced
1/3 cup fresh parsley, minced
4 ounces Feta cheese, crumbled
1 teaspoon dried dill weed
1/2 teaspoon nutmeg
1 teaspoon salt
1/2 teaspoon pepper

Add remaining ingredients through pepper. Turn machine on "cake" cycle. After the 30 minute "stirring" period, check to make sure mixture is combined and top is flattened. Remove after 1 hour 35 minutes from beginning of cycle or when a sharp knife inserted in the center comes out clean. Be careful, pan is very hot! (The machine's baking cycle will not necessarily be completed.)

* Unmold. Cool slightly. Cut into 8 slices with a sharp knife. Cut each slice into 8 squares.

1 1/2 cups commercial chunky salsa

Top each square with a generous teaspoon of salsa.

Serve warm or at room temperature. Serve large slices (soften onion in vegetable broth instead of chicken broth) for a delightful vegetarian main dish.

28% calories from fat per serving

Yield: 16 (4-piece) servings

Nutrient content per serving:

Calories: 76   Fat: 2.4 g   Protein: 6.2 g   Carbohydrate: 7.5 g

Sodium: 477.7 mg   Cholesterol: 35.4 mg   Fiber: 2.8 g

Alternate Method: Soften onion by "sauteing" in broth in a small saucepan for about 5 minutes. Puree onion, spinach and eggs. Combine with remaining ingredients in a large mixing bowl. Pour into a 9x5x3-inch loaf pan which has been sprayed with nonstick cooking spray. Bake in a preheated 350 degree oven for about 1 hour to 1 hour 15 minutes or until a sharp knife inserted in the center comes out clean. Continue from * above.

Gazpacho Ice

Don't limit your ice cream machine to desserts! Almost fat-free and loaded with vitamins, this is a healthy start to a summer evening.

1/3 cup parsley
2 garlic cloves, peeled
1/2 cup red onions, coarsely
   chopped
1/2 cup green pepper, coarsely
   chopped
1 (14 1/2-ounce) can plum tomatoes,
   drained (reserve liquid)

1 cup vegetable juice
1/3 cup commercial, fat-free,
   Italian dressing
1 teaspoon Worcestershire sauce
1 teaspoon salt

* Mince parsley and garlic in a food processor or a blender. Add onion and green pepper and process by turning machine on and off until vegetables are finely chopped, but not pureed. Add tomatoes. Turn machine on and off quickly once or twice or until tomatoes are chopped. (Or chop in small batches in a blender.)

Combine vegetables with remaining ingredients and reserved tomato liquid and freeze in the **ice cream machine** according to manufacturer's instructions. The ice is finished when it is the consistency of a sorbet. Store in the freezer until serving time.

Remove from freezer about 15 minutes before serving to soften slightly. If you don't want to freeze it, serve chilled as gazpacho soup!

2% calories from fat per serving

Yield: 6 (2/3-cup) servings
Nutrient content per serving:
Calories: 40   Fat: 0.1 g   Protein: 1.4 g   Carbohydrate: 8.4 g
Sodium: 796.6 mg   Cholesterol: 0.0 mg   Fiber: 1.7 g

Alternate Method: Prepare vegetables as * above. Pour combined ingredients into a 9x9x2-inch metal pan. Cover and put in freezer, about 3 hours total. When tomato mixture begins to freeze around the edge of pan, stir, and return to freezer for several more hours.

Marinated Shrimp

Use the heatproof oven bag and the microwave for a quick no mess effort. Best of all - no fishy smell!

12 ounces medium-size raw shrimp, peeled, deveined and tail removed
1 lemon, washed, sliced thin
1/2 cup red onion, sliced thin
1/4 cup fresh parsley, minced
1/2 cup commercial fat-free Italian dressing

Place shrimp in a **heatproof oven bag** and place bag in a **microwave**-safe dish. (If your heatproof oven bag requires the use of flour, refer to the Special notes on pages 14 and 15.) Tie and vent according to package directions. Microwave on high for about 3 minutes total or until shrimp are just pink and firm. (Shake bag carefully and turn over halfway through cooking.) Rest 5 minutes. Drain any liquid in the oven bag and let shrimp cool. * Transfer shrimp to a heavy-duty zip-top plastic food storage bag and add remaining ingredients. Marinate refrigerated 24-48 hours, tossing periodically.

lemon wedges
shredded lettuce

Transfer shrimp to a platter with a slotted spoon. Garnish with lemon wedges and shredded lettuce.

1% calories from fat per serving

Yield: 4 (3-ounce) servings
Nutrient content per serving:
Calories: 99   Fat: 0.1 g   Protein: 17.7 g   Carbohydrate: 6.9 g
Sodium: 886.5 mg   Cholesterol: 137.2 mg   Fiber: 0.5 g

Alternate Methods:
Microwave in a casserole: Place shrimp in a microwave-safe casserole. Cover tightly. Cook at high for 4 to 6 minutes. Rest 5 minutes. Drain. Cool. Continue from * above.

Stovetop: Bring 4 cups of water to a boil in a large saucepan. Add shrimp and return to a boil, reduce to a simmer and cook covered for 3 to 5 minutes or until shrimp are tender. Drain. Cool. Continue from * above.

Roasted Eggplant Dip

This garlicky dip is not for the faint of heart. Use one clove of garlic if you're in doubt! The heatproof oven bag frees you of a messy baking pan to clean as well as retaining more moisture in the eggplant.

1 (1 1/2-pound) eggplant
1/2 cup plain fat-free yogurt
1/4 cup grated Parmesan cheese
3 garlic cloves
1 tablespoon lemon juice
1 teaspoon dried oregano leaves
1/2 teaspoon salt
1/8 teaspoon pepper

Preheat oven to 375 degrees. Halve eggplant lengthwise. Place halves in a **heatproof oven bag** and place the oven bag in a baking pan. (If your heatproof oven bag requires the use of flour, refer to the Special notes on pages 14 and 15.) Tie and vent according to package directions. Bake, cut sides down, for about 40 minutes or until the eggplant is very soft. Slit the oven bag and allow the eggplant to cool. * Remove and discard the seeds and scrape the flesh from the skin. Puree eggplant flesh and remaining ingredients in a food processor. (Or puree small batches in a blender.) Chill until serving time.

Serve warm or cold with toasted pita bread. This is also a wonderful dressing on freshly steamed vegetables. Use fat-free Parmesan cheese, if desired.

18% calories from fat per serving

Yield: 8 (2-ounce) servings
Nutrient content per serving:
Calories: 49   Fat: 1.0 g   Protein: 2.6 g   Carbohydrate: 7.4 g
Sodium: 206.5 mg   Cholesterol: 2.6 mg   Fiber: 0.1 g

Alternate Method: Spray a baking pan with nonstick cooking spray. Place eggplant in baking pan, cut sides down, and bake for 50 to 60 minutes or until eggplant is very soft. Allow eggplant to cool. Continue from * above.

Black Bean and Chick Pea Dip

Using dried beans reduces sodium by a whopping 60 percent, but for ease, canned beans can be used. See alternate method.

2/3 cup dried garbanzo beans,
  (chick-peas)
2/3 cup dried black beans
1/2 cup fat-free sour cream
5 teaspoons olive oil
2 garlic cloves, minced
2 1/2 tablespoons lemon juice
3/4 teaspoon salt
1/4 teaspoon white pepper

Place dried beans in a bowl, cover with water and soak overnight or for at least 8 hours. Drain. Place in the **slow cooker** with 3 cups water and cook on high temperature for about 4 hours or until beans are very tender. Drain. * Puree beans and remaining ingredients in a food processor. (Or puree small batches in a blender.) Prepare at least 8 hours in advance for flavors to blend. Refrigerate until serving.

Serve with chips or crackers.

23% calories from fat per serving

Yield: 12 (2-ounce) servings (3 cups)
Nutrient content per serving:
Calories: 104   Fat: 2.7 g   Protein: 5.7 g   Carbohydrate: 14.2 g
Sodium: 160.4 mg   Cholesterol: 0.0 mg   Fiber: 3.6 g

Alternate Method: Use 1 (15-ounce) can garbanzo beans, drained and rinsed, and 1 (15-ounce) can black beans, drained and rinsed, in place of dried beans. Continue from * above, reducing amount of sour cream to 1/4 cup plus 2 tablespoons.

Spicy Dried Fruit Mix

Use the heatproof oven bag and avoid watching and stirring. The small amount of included oil is not left on the baking pan, but used to its full extent to add flavor to the mix.

1/2 cup crispy rice noodles
1/2 cup plus 2 tablespoons raisins
1/2 cup plus 2 tablespoons dried cranberries
1 1/2 tablespoons vegetable oil
1 tablespoon dry sherry or apple juice
1/2 teaspoon salt
1/2 teaspoon ground ginger
1/2 teaspoon ground cloves
1/8 teaspoon cayenne pepper

* Preheat oven to 300 degrees. Combine noodles, raisins, and cranberries in a **heatproof oven bag**. Toss. Add remaining ingredients. Toss again. Let stand 15 minutes. (If your heatproof oven bag requires the use of flour, refer to the Special notes on pages 14 and 15.) Tie and vent oven bag according to package directions. Place oven bag in a baking pan and spread raisin mixture into an even layer. Bake for 15 minutes. ** Pour onto paper towels to cool.

Do you like it HOT? Use more cayenne.

24% calories from fat per serving

Yield: 6 (1/4-cup) servings
Nutrient content per serving:
Calories: 164   Fat: 4.4 g   Protein: 0.9 g   Carbohydrate: 30.1 g
Sodium: 269.1 mg   Cholesterol: 0.0 mg   Fiber: 1.6 g

Alternate Method: Prepare as * above tossing ingredients in a plastic food storage bag instead of a heatproof oven bag. Empty into a foil-lined baking pan. Bake for 15 minutes, tossing gently, every 5 minutes. Continue from ** above.

Peppered Corn Chips

Use this technique to season purchased chips to suit your taste. Baked with seasoning, chips are flakier. Best warm, enjoy anytime!

2 teaspoons vegetable oil
4 teaspoons water
4 ounces plain, low-fat corn chips
   (if large, break into 1-inch pieces)
1/4 teaspoon red pepper flakes
1 teaspoon paprika
1/2 teaspoon garlic powder
1/2 teaspoon onion powder

* Preheat oven to 300 degrees. Whisk oil and water in a small dish until combined. Place chips in a **heatproof oven bag**, add water and oil mixture and toss gently. Combine pepper flakes through onion powder and sprinkle evenly over chips in oven bag. Toss gently so chips are covered evenly. Let stand for 5 minutes. Toss again gently. (If your heatproof oven bag requires the use of flour, refer to the Special notes on pages 14 and 15.) Tie and vent according to package directions and place oven bag in a baking pan, distributing chips. Bake for 5 minutes. Turn over carefully. ** Bake 5 minutes more or until chips have turned a delicate, golden color. Serve warm or at room temperature.

Toss and bake in the same heatproof oven bag: less oil, no cleanup!

22% calories from fat per serving

Yield: 6 servings
Nutrient content per serving:
Calories: 90   Fat: 2.2 g   Protein: 2.1 g   Carbohydrate: 15.4 g
Sodium: 95.2 mg   Cholesterol: 0.0 mg   Fiber: 1.4 g

Alternate Method: Prepare as * above tossing ingredients in a plastic food storage bag instead of a heatproof oven bag. Empty chips into a foil-lined baking pan. (Separate chips, if necessary.) Bake for about 5 minutes. Turn chips over. Continue from ** above. More oil may be required using this method since some liquid will cling to the food storage bag.

Crab Puffs

Store these morsels in the freezer in the heatproof oven bag, then bake them in the same oven bag for a no mess treat.

6 ounces fat-free cream cheese, softened
1/4 cup fat-free mayonnaise
1/4 cup light sour cream (not fat-free)
1 (6-ounce) can crabmeat, drained
1/2 teaspoon onion powder
1 garlic clove, minced
3/4 teaspoon Worcestershire sauce
1/4 teaspoon red pepper flakes
2 tablespoons parsley, minced

10 thin slices white bread, crusts removed, cut into quarters

* Combine first three ingredients and blend well. Add crabmeat through parsley and combine.

** Place 2 **heatproof oven bags** on two cookie sheets. Arrange 20 bread squares on **top** of each oven bag. Divide crab mixture among bread squares. Freeze. When frozen solid, place crab puffs **in** the oven bag. Tie. Keep frozen until needed. (If your heatproof oven bag requires the use of flour, refer to the Special notes on pages 14 and 15.) Just before baking, tie and vent oven bag according to package directions and place the oven bag in a baking pan. Arrange puffs so cheese sides are "up". Bake **frozen** puffs in a preheated 400 degree oven for 10 to 12 minutes or until bread is lightly toasted and cheese just begins to bubble. Slit oven bag to remove puffs.

These are terrific for lunch; prepare as above but don't quarter the bread slices.

19% calories from fat per puff

Yield: 40 crab puffs
Nutrient content per puff:
Calories: 71   Fat: 1.5 g   Protein: 5.9 g   Carbohydrate: 8.5 g
Sodium: 250.1 mg   Cholesterol: 15.9 mg   Fiber: 0.3 g

Alternate Method: Combine ingredients as * above and divide crab mixture among bread squares. Place puffs on cookie sheets and broil 6 inches from heat for about 3 minutes or until tops are lightly browned and bubbly. If preparing ahead, freeze directly on cookie sheets, then store in heavy-duty zip-top plastic storage bags. To prepare, **remove from storage bags, defrost,** then broil.

Blue Cheesy Potatoes

Served hot or at room temperature, these are quick and light.

12 small round red potatoes (about 1 pound)

Place potatoes in a circle on a **microwave**-safe plate. Add 2 tablespoons water. Cover lightly. Cook on high for about 7 minutes or until the tip of a sharp knife cuts the potato easily. (Rotate plate 1/2 turn halfway through cooking time if microwave does not have a carousel.) Rest for 5 minutes.

2 tablespoons blue cheese, crumbled
1/4 cup plain nonfat yogurt
1 tablespoon minced green onions
1/8 teaspoon red pepper flakes, crushed
1/4 teaspoon salt

* Meanwhile, combine cheese through salt. Cut potatoes lengthwise. (If necessary, cut a tiny slice from the bottom so potatoes will not wobble.) Top each potato with a scant teaspoon of cheese mixture.

paprika

Sprinkle with paprika.

7% calories from fat per potato half

Yield: 24 potato halves
Nutrient content per potato half:
Calories: 27   Fat: 0.2 g   Protein: 0.8 g   Carbohydrate: 5.4 g
Sodium: 35.9 mg   Cholesterol: 0.5 mg   Fiber: 0.0 g

Alternate Method: Cook potatoes in boiling water to cover for 15 to 20 minutes or until just tender. Drain. Continue from * above.

Curried Corn In Pumpkin Cups

Bread cups are so easy and so good. These just look like fall. Invent your own to fit the season!

6 slices Pumpkin Bread with Dried Cranberries (page 46), sliced 1/2-inch thick
mini-muffin pans, 1 1/2-inch diameter
1/2 cup frozen corn, thawed and drained
3 tablespoons fat-free sour cream
1 teaspoon curry powder
1 tablespoon fresh cilantro, minced
1/2 teaspoon salt

Preheat oven to 400 degrees. Remove crusts from bread. Flatten with a rolling pin. Cut each into 4 squares. Spray squares lightly with nonstick cooking spray. Spray mini-muffin pans. Carefully press a bread square into each muffin cup. Bake for 5 minutes or until lightly browned. Meanwhile, combine corn through salt in a small bowl. Fill each bread cup with a generous teaspoon of the corn mixture. Bake 2 minutes or until warm.

Make bread cups ahead, if desired. These cups can be made with commercial white bread.

13% calories from fat per cup

Yield: 24 cups

Nutrient content per cup:

Calories: 69   Fat: 1.0 g   Protein: 1.8 g   Carbohydrate: 13.2 g
Sodium: 113.5 mg   Cholesterol: 5.4 mg   Fiber: 0.9 g

Jalapeño, Jalapeño, Jalapeño Cups

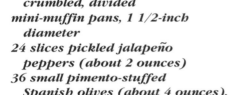

If you like these fiery peppers, this snack is for you! Bread cups can be made ahead, then filled and reheated at the last minute.

6 slices Jalapeño Bread (page 39),
   about 1/2-inch thick
1 teaspoon chili powder, divided
1 teaspoon dried basil leaves,
   crumbled, divided
mini-muffin pans, 1 1/2-inch
   diameter
24 slices pickled jalapeño
   peppers (about 2 ounces)
36 small pimento-stuffed
   Spanish olives (about 4 ounces),
   halved
1/4 cup jalapeño pepper jelly,
   divided

Preheat oven to 400 degrees. Remove crusts from bread. Flatten with a rolling pin. Cut each into 4 squares. Spray squares lightly with nonstick cooking spray. Sprinkle with chili powder and basil. Spray mini-muffin pans. Carefully press a bread square into each muffin cup. Bake for 5 minutes or until lightly browned. Cool slightly. Into each bread cup, place 1 pepper slice and 3 olive halves. Top with 1/2 teaspoon jelly. Bake 2 minutes more or until warm.

*Create your own bread cups and fillings. With the **bread machine**, there's no limit to your creativity. These cups can be made with commercial white bread.*

21% calories from fat per cup

Yield: 24 cups
Nutrient content per cup:
Calories: 64   Fat: 1.5 g   Protein: 1.5 g   Carbohydrate: 11.0 g
Sodium: 256.2 mg   Cholesterol: 0.0 mg   Fiber: 0.2 g

Bread

Notes

--------------------------------- ---------------------------------
--------------------------------- ---------------------------------
--------------------------------- ---------------------------------
--------------------------------- ---------------------------------
--------------------------------- ---------------------------------
--------------------------------- ---------------------------------
--------------------------------- ---------------------------------
--------------------------------- ---------------------------------
--------------------------------- ---------------------------------
--------------------------------- ---------------------------------
--------------------------------- ---------------------------------
--------------------------------- ---------------------------------
--------------------------------- ---------------------------------
--------------------------------- ---------------------------------

Jalapeño Bread

Toasted and spread with fat-free cream cheese..., yum!

1 1/4 cups water
2 tablespoons olive oil
3 1/2 cups bread flour
1/2 cup oatmeal, "quick" type
2 tablespoons nonfat dry skim milk
2 tablespoons sugar
2 teaspoons ground cumin
1 teaspoon dried coriander leaves, crumbled
1/4 teaspoon garlic powder
1 teaspoon salt
2 teaspoons active dry yeast

Combine all ingredients up to jalapeño slices in **automatic bread machine** in the order specified by the manufacturer. Set on "raisin bread" cycle.

1/2 cup pickled jalapeño slices

Add the jalapeño slices at the beep. (Push dough down sides quickly with a spatula to make sure slices are incorporated.)

14% calories from fat per serving

Yield: 12 servings
Nutrient content per serving:
Calories: 191   Fat: 3.0 g   Protein: 5.9 g   Carbohydrate: 35.0 g
Sodium: 338.7 mg   Cholesterol: 0.1 mg   Fiber: 0.7 g

Alternate Method: Follow manual breadmaking instructions on page 233.

Olive Bread

Bet you didn't think an olive bread could be included in a low-fat cookbook.

1/2 cup plus 2 tablespoons water
1 1/2 tablespoons olive oil
1 1/2 cups bread flour
2 1/2 tablespoons dry skim milk
3/4 teaspoon salt
1/4 cup Calamata olives, pitted, minced (about 12 olives)
1 teaspoon active dry yeast

Combine all ingredients in **automatic bread machine** in the order specified by the manufacturer. Set on "bread" cycle or set the timer for a later start.

For larger pieces of olives in this bread, set on raisin bread cycle and add olives at the beep.

30% calories from fat per serving

Yield: 6 servings
Nutrient content per serving:
Calories: 189   Fat: 6.4 g   Protein: 5.0 g   Carbohydrate: 27.8 g
Sodium: 482.1 mg   Cholesterol: 0.3 mg   Fiber: 0.3 g

Alternate Method: Follow manual breadmaking instructions on page 233.

Chocolate Chip Banana Bread

Chocoholics - you don't have to feel guilty eating this bread.

3/4 cup plus 2 tablespoons plain nonfat yogurt
1 tablespoon vegetable oil
1 teaspoon vanilla
1 cup (2 medium) mashed ripe bananas (be sure to measure)
3 cups bread flour
2 tablespoons sugar
3/4 teaspoon salt
1 1/2 teaspoons active dry yeast

1/2 cup plus 1 tablespoon semi-sweet chocolate chips, frozen for at least 2 hours

Strain yogurt (see instructions on page 235) for 10 minutes or until about 1 ounce has drained. Discard liquid. Combine all ingredients up to chips in **automatic bread machine** in the order specified by the manufacturer. Set on "raisin bread" cycle.

Add frozen chips at the beep. (Push dough down sides quickly with a spatula to make sure chips are incorporated.)

When bread is finished, allow to cool for 30 minutes for easier slicing.

This bread is so luscious, you could almost serve it for dessert!

17% calories from fat per serving

Yield: 10 servings
Nutrient content per serving:
Calories: 268   Fat: 5.0 g   Protein: 7.4 g   Carbohydrate: 48.4 g
Sodium: 192.4 mg   Cholesterol: 0.9 mg   Fiber: 1.3 g

Alternate Method: Follow manual breadmaking instructions on page 233.

Focaccia Bread with Onions

This is more like a pizza than a bread. In fact, it's a meal in itself. But, it's oh, so light!

3/4 cup water
2 tablespoons vegetable oil
2 cups bread flour
1 teaspoon sugar
1 teaspoon dried oregano leaves
1 teaspoon salt
1 teaspoon active dry yeast

Combine water through yeast in **automatic bread machine** in the order specified by the manufacturer. Set on "dough" cycle.

10-inch diameter round baking pan

* When cycle has completed, transfer dough to a floured surface and punch down with floured hands on a floured surface. Roll into a circle slightly larger than the baking pan. Spray the pan with nonstick cooking spray. Place the dough in the pan, pushing up the sides of the pan slightly. Cover with a clean cloth and let it rise in a warm, draft-free spot for about 1 hour or until a finger leaves a dent in the dough.

1 cup onion, halved, thinly sliced
*   crosswise*
2 garlic cloves, minced
1 teaspoon dried rosemary leaves
1 tablespoon oil

Meanwhile, combine onion through oil in a **microwave**-safe dish. Cook, uncovered, on high for 3 minutes. Stir. Cook another 3 minutes, stir, then cook another 2 minutes, or until onions are tender and lightly browned. (Careful, do not burn.)

2 tablespoons Parmesan cheese,
*   grated*
freshly ground pepper

** Preheat oven to 400 degrees. Make indentations 1 inch apart on dough pressing almost to the bottom of the pan. Top with the onion mixture. Brush the dough with the pan juices to moisten. Sprinkle with cheese and pepper. Bake for 22 to 25 minutes or until lightly browned. Remove to a wire rack for bottom to crisp.

Let your imagination soar and top with almost anything; but watch calories and fat content. To lower fat percentage, use fat-free Parmesan cheese.

28% calories from fat per serving

Yield: 10 servings

Nutrient content per serving:

Calories: 149   Fat: 4.7 g   Protein: 4.1 g   Carbohydrate: 22.6 g
Sodium: 253.1 mg   Cholesterol: 0.8 mg   Fiber: 0.5 g

Alternate Method: Follow manual breadmaking instructions on page 233. Instead of forming into a loaf shape, continue as * above. Cook onions and garlic in rosemary and oil in a skillet until tender and lightly browned. Continue from ** above.

Oatmeal Bread

A light, healthy bread to wake up to.

1 1/4 cups water
1 cup oatmeal, "quick" type
2 1/2 cups bread flour
1/4 cup brown sugar
1/4 cup buttermilk powder
2 tablespoons margarine
1/2 teaspoon salt
1 1/2 teaspoons active dry yeast

Combine all ingredients in **automatic bread machine** in the order specified by the manufacturer. Set on "bread" cycle or set the timer for a later start.

Best warm or toasted – pass the jam!

14% calories from fat per serving

Yield: 10 servings

Nutrient content per serving:

Calories: 207   Fat: 3.3 g   Protein: 6.6 g   Carbohydrate: 37.6 g
Sodium: 166.7 mg   Cholesterol: 2.1 mg   Fiber: 0.7 g

Alternate Method: Follow manual breadmaking instructions on page 233.

Prune Bread

A breakfast bread with just a hint of prune flavor, despite the fairly large amount in the recipe.

1 1/4 cups water
1 tablespoon vegetable oil
1 cup whole wheat flour
2 cups bread flour
2 tablespoons brown sugar, packed
2 tablespoons sugar
1 teaspoon salt
1 cup chopped pitted prunes, loosely packed
1 1/2 teaspoons active dry yeast

Combine all ingredients in **automatic bread machine** in the order specified by the manufacturer. Set on "bread" cycle or set the timer for a later start.

The finished bread does not have visible prune pieces since they are included with the other ingredients at the start of the cycle. If a "chunkier" result is desired, set on "raisin bread" cycle and add prunes at the beep.

8% calories from fat per serving

Yield: 10 servings
Nutrient content per serving:
Calories: 218   Fat: 2.0 g   Protein: 5.6 g   Carbohydrate: 44.4 g
Sodium: 236.6 mg   Cholesterol: 0.0 mg   Fiber: 2.9 g

Alternate Method: Follow manual breadmaking instructions on page 233.

Pumpkin Bread With Dried Cranberries

Don't save this bread for Thanksgiving. It's so easy, anytime is a good time.

*3/4 cup plus 2 tablespoons canned
    pumpkin
1 egg
2 tablespoons vegetable oil
1 (2 1/2-ounce) jar prune puree
    (baby food containing no tapioca)
1/2 cup water
2 cups bread flour
1 cup whole wheat flour
1/4 cup brown sugar, packed
2 tablespoons nonfat dry skim milk
1/4 teaspoon ground cloves
1/4 teaspoon ground nutmeg
1 teaspoon salt
1 1/2 teaspoons active dry yeast*

*1/2 cup dried cranberries
1 teaspoon flour*

Combine all ingredients up to cranberries in **automatic bread machine** in the order specified by the manufacturer. Set on "raisin bread" cycle.

Meanwhile, combine cranberries and flour by tossing in a small plastic bag. At the beep, add the cranberries and flour. (Push dough down sides quickly with a spatula to make sure cranberries are incorporated.)

14% calories from fat per serving

Yield: 10 servings
Nutrient content per serving:
Calories: 254   Fat: 3.9 g   Protein: 6.4 g   Carbohydrate: 48.3 g
Sodium: 252.7 mg   Cholesterol: 21.4 mg   Fiber: 3.1 g

Alternate Method: Follow manual breadmaking instructions on page 233.

Herb Bread with Cornmeal

Set the machine's timer in the morning; enjoy this savory bread for dinner.

3/4 cup water
1 tablespoon vegetable oil
2 cups bread flour
1/4 cup white or yellow cornmeal
1 tablespoon sugar
3 tablespoons dry skim milk
1 teaspoon salt
1 teaspoon dried thyme leaves, crumbled
1 teaspoon dried rosemary leaves, crumbled
1 1/2 teaspoons active dry yeast

Combine all ingredients in **automatic bread machine** in the order specified by the manufacturer. Set on "bread" cycle or set the timer for a later start.

12% calories from fat per serving

Yield: 8 servings

Nutrient content per serving:
Calories: 167   Fat: 2.2 g   Protein: 5.3 g   Carbohydrate: 31.5 g
Sodium: 301.4 mg   Cholesterol: 0.3 mg   Fiber: 0.7 g

Alternate Method: Follow manual breadmaking instructions on page 233.

Cranberry Bread

A very moist, dense bread. Pass a bowl of cranberry sauce for a double cranberry taste treat.

1/2 cup water
1 1/2 teaspoons almond extract
1 1/4 cups whole berry cranberry sauce
3 cups bread flour
2 tablespoons sugar
1/2 teaspoon salt
2 tablespoons margarine
2 1/2 teaspoons active dry yeast

Combine all ingredients up to raisins in **automatic bread machine** in the order specified by the manufacturer. Set on "raisin bread" cycle.

1/2 cup raisins
1/2 cup water

Meanwhile, plump raisins by combining with water in **microwave**-safe bowl. Cover. Microwave on high for 3 minutes. Drain. Add raisins to bread machine at the "beep". (Push dough down sides quickly with a spatula to make sure raisins are incorporated into dough.)

10% calories from fat per serving

Yield: 10 servings
Nutrient content per serving:
Calories: 258   Fat: 2.8 g   Protein: 5.6 g   Carbohydrate: 52.5 g
Sodium: 129.0 mg   Cholesterol: 0.0 mg   Fiber: 1.1 g

Alternate Method: Follow manual breadmaking instructions on page 233. Cover raisins with water in a small saucepan and simmer, covered, for 10 minutes to plump. Drain.

Herbed Garlic Bread

Keep this bread in the freezer for a no-mess, last-minute treat!

1/4 cup plus 2 tablespoons fresh parsley, minced
1 egg white, lightly beaten
3 garlic cloves, minced
1 1/2 tablespoons olive oil
1 (8-ounce) loaf French bread, halved and split lengthwise
4 teaspoons Parmesan cheese, grated
1/2 teaspoon Seed Rub (page 208)

* Combine parsley through oil in a small bowl. Spread mixture on cut sides of bread. Sprinkle with cheese and Seed Rub. Place 2 bread halves in 2 **heatproof oven bags**. Tie. Freeze. When ready to bake, preheat oven to 350 degrees. (If your heatproof oven bag requires the use of flour, refer to the Special notes on pages 14 and 15.) Tie and vent according to package directions. Place frozen bread in the oven bag, cheese side up, in a baking pan and bake for 18 to 20 minutes or until top is set and edges are lightly browned. Slit oven bag open immediately. ** Cut each loaf half into thirds.

30% calories from fat per serving

Yield: 12 servings

Nutrient content per serving:

Calories: 72   Fat: 2.4 g   Protein: 2.3 g   Carbohydrate: 10.3 g
Sodium: 132.9 mg   Cholesterol: 0.4 mg   Fiber: 0.6 g

Alternate Method: Prepare bread as * above. To freeze, place in heavy-duty zip-top plastic storage bags. To bake, **remove from storage bags, defrost,** then place directly on cookie sheets and bake in a preheated, 350 degree oven for 15 to 18 minutes or until top is set and edges are lightly browned. Continue as ** above.

Rye Bread With Beer

Serve this with baked beans; especially good warm topped with yogurt cheese.

3/4 cup plus 2 tablespoons beer
1/3 cup dark molasses
2 tablespoons vegetable oil
1/2 cup whole wheat flour
1 1/3 cups rye flour
1 cup bread flour
1/2 teaspoon salt
1 1/2 teaspoons active dry yeast

Let beer go "flat" by allowing it to sit at room temperature for at least 15 minutes. Then combine all ingredients in **automatic bread machine** in the order specified by the manufacturer. Set on "bread" cycle or set the timer for a later start.

17% calories from fat per serving

Yield: 10 servings
Nutrient content per serving:
Calories: 170   Fat: 3.2 g   Protein: 4.0 g   Carbohydrate: 31.2 g
Sodium: 128.1 mg   Cholesterol: 0.0 mg   Fiber: 2.9 g

Alternate Method: Follow manual breadmaking instructions on page 233.

Soups and Stews

Soups and Stews

Notes

_____   _____
_____   _____
_____   _____
_____   _____
_____   _____
_____   _____
_____   _____
_____   _____
_____   _____
_____   _____
_____   _____
_____   _____
_____   _____
_____   _____

Lamb Soup With Orzo

A hearty soup for a cold, winter's eve.

**1 pound lean boneless lamb, all
  fat trimmed, cut into 1-inch cubes**
8 cups water
**3 large carrots, peeled and cut into
  2-inch pieces**
4 stalks celery, cut into 2-inch pieces
1 large onion, quartered
1 bay leaf
1/2 teaspoon garlic powder
1 1/2 teaspoons dried basil leaves
1 teaspoon salt
1/4 teaspoon pepper

1 cup orzo (rice-shaped) pasta

Combine lamb through pepper in the
slow cooker. Cook on high for 5
hours or on low for 10 hours or until
meat and vegetables are very tender.
Discard bay leaf. Remove vegetables
and puree in a food processor. (Or
puree small batches in a blender.)

Return pureed vegetables to slow
cooker along with pasta and cook on
high for 1 hour or until pasta is very
tender. Stir at least twice during this
period. (Simmer on stovetop 25 minutes, if desired.) Skim all fat before
serving. (Quick tip: Drop a few ice
cubes in soup, fat will congeal to ice.
Immediately remove cubes.)

Add additional salt to taste.

21% calories from fat per serving

Yield: 14 (1-cup) servings
Nutrient content per serving:
Calories: 122   Fat: 2.8 g   Protein: 11.2 g   Carbohydrate: 13.0 g
Sodium: 204.2 mg   Cholesterol: 28.9 mg   Fiber: 1.5 g

Alternate Method: Combine lamb through pepper in a large soup pot. Bring to a boil, reduce heat, and
simmer, covered, for 2 hours or until meat and vegetables are very tender. Discard bay leaf. Puree vegetables
and return to the soup pot with pasta. Simmer covered for 25 minutes or until pasta is very tender. Stir occasionally. Skim fat before serving.

Pumpkin Soup with Spinach

This simple soup is high in nutrients and low in fat. Pumpkin is a good source of vitamin A with 1536 RE/serving!

1/2 cup onion, chopped
2 cups chicken broth, defatted, divided
1 cup canned pumpkin
1/2 cup chopped frozen spinach (use "loose pack")
1/2 cup unsweetened applesauce
1/4 teaspoon nutmeg
1/2 teaspoon salt
1/8 teaspoon white pepper

Place onion and 1/2 cup of the broth in a 2-quart microwave-safe bowl. Cover. Cook in the **microwave** at high temperature for about 2 minutes or until softened. Add remaining ingredients (including remaining broth) and combine. Cover tightly and cook at high for 5 minutes. Stir. Cook 5 minutes more. Let rest 5 minutes before serving.

"Loose pack" spinach is available in plastic bags in the freezer section.

4% calories from fat per serving

Yield: 4 (1-cup) servings

Nutrient content per serving:

Calories: 72   Fat: 0.3 g   Protein: 4.8 g   Carbohydrate: 12.4 g

Sodium: 324.1 mg   Cholesterol: 0.0 mg   Fiber: 3.4 g

Alternate Method: Combine onions with 1/2 cup of the broth in a saucepan. Cover and cook on low for about 10 minutes or until onions are softened. Add remaining ingredients (including remaining broth). Bring to a boil, reduce to a simmer and cook, covered, for about 15 minutes. Stir at least twice.

Minestrone

Comfort food!

1 pound lean, top round of beef, cut
   into 1/2-inch cubes
1 1/2 cups onion, chopped
1 garlic clove, minced
1 (14 1/2-ounce) can diced tomatoes
2 cups beef broth, defatted
2 cups vegetable broth or juice
1/2 cup red wine
1 1/2 cups water
1 bay leaf
1/2 teaspoon dried rosemary leaves
1 teaspoon dried thyme leaves
1/2 teaspoon ground celery seed
1 teaspoon salt
1/4 teaspoon pepper

Combine beef through pepper in the
slow cooker. Cover and cook on low
for 7 to 8 hours or until meat is tender.

1 cup elbow macaroni
2 cups frozen mixed vegetables

Turn heat to high, add macaroni and
vegetables, and cook for 30 to 40
minutes or until macaroni is just tender.

1 (1-pound) can white kidney beans,
   drained and rinsed

Add beans and cook on high for an
additional 5 minutes or until beans are
warmed. Remove bay leaf. Correct
seasoning, if desired.

*Imported pasta produces a better result in a
slow cooker. Generally, the durum wheat is
"harder", so the pasta is not "mushy".*

13% calories from fat per serving

Yield: 10 (1 1/2-cup) servings
Nutrient content per serving:
Calories: 231   Fat: 3.3 g   Protein: 22.2 g   Carbohydrate: 26.2 g
Sodium: 700 mg   Cholesterol: 41.3 mg   Fiber: 4.5 g   Alcohol: 1.1 g

Alternate Method: Coat a large soup pot with nonstick cooking spray. Add meat through garlic and cook
until meat loses pink color. Add remaining ingredients through pepper, bring to a boil, cover, reduce to a simmer, and cook for 1 to 1 1/2 hours or until meat is tender. Add macaroni, vegetables and beans and cook for
10 minutes or until macaroni is just tender. Remove bay leaf. Correct seasoning, if desired.

Lentil Soup With Potatoes and Spinach

Lentils produce their own broth, are the fastest cooking dried beans, are high in protein, complex carbohydrates and fiber, and contain almost no fat. Is this a perfect food or what?

1 cup brown lentils
1 cup onions, chopped
2 cups potatoes, peeled, and cut into 1/2-inch cubes
3 cups frozen cut leaf spinach ("loose pack")
3 tablespoons low-sodium tomato paste
1 tablespoon vegetable oil
5 1/2 cups water
1 teaspoon curry powder
3/4 teaspoon ground cumin
1/2 teaspoon ground ginger
1 teaspoon salt

1/2 cup fat-free sour cream

Combine lentils through salt in the **slow cooker**. Cook at low temperature for 8 to 10 hours or until lentils and vegetables are tender.

Serve in bowls, top with 1 tablespoon sour cream.

10% calories from fat per serving

Yield: 8 (1-cup) servings
Nutrient content per serving:
Calories: 209   Fat: 2.3 g   Protein: 11.5 g   Carbohydrate: 35.5 g
Sodium: 379.8 mg   Cholesterol: 0.0 mg   Fiber: 11.1 g

Alternate Method: Combine lentils through salt in a large soup pot. Bring to a boil, reduce to a simmer and cook, covered, for 1 hour or until lentils and vegetables are tender. Stir occasionally.

Chicken Soup with Rice and Barley

An "almost" old-fashioned chicken soup doesn't require the old-fashioned attention.

4 (5-ounce) chicken breasts, bone-in, skin removed
1 cup carrots, coarsely chopped
2 cups onion, coarsely chopped
3 cups chicken broth, defatted
4 cups water
2 chicken bouillon cubes
1/2 teaspoon pepper

Place chicken breasts, bone side up, in the **slow cooker**. Add remaining ingredients through pepper. Cook on low for 7 to 8 hours or until a fork pierces meat easily. * Remove chicken and vegetables. Puree vegetables in a food processor. (Or puree small batches in a blender.) Skim all fat from broth. Bone chicken and cut into small pieces.

1/2 cup long-grain white rice
1/4 cup medium barley
1 teaspoon dried thyme leaves

Return broth and pureed vegetables to the slow cooker and add rice, barley and thyme. Cover and cook at high for about 1 hour and 15 minutes or until rice and barley are very tender. Add chicken during the last 15 minutes.

7% calories from fat per serving

Yield: 8 (1 1/2-cup) servings
Nutrient content per serving:
Calories: 191   Fat: 1.4 g   Protein: 24.1 g   Carbohydrate: 20.5 g
Sodium: 251.3 mg   Cholesterol: 49.4 mg   Fiber: 2.2 g

Alternate Method: Combine ingredients through pepper in a soup pot, bring to a boil, reduce to a simmer, and cook, covered, for about 1 1/2 hours or until meat tests done. Stir occasionally. Continue from * above, then return ingredients to the soup pot and cook for about 50 minutes or until rice and barley are tender. Stir frequently during this period. Add chicken during the last 10 minutes.

15 Bean Soup

A no effort bean soup; so good for you, too!

2 cups dried beans,
  "15 varieties"
6 cups water

Place beans and 6 cups water in a **slow cooker**, cover, and cook on low overnight or for at least 8 hours. Drain.

3 1/2 cups water
1 1/2 cups coarsely chopped
  onions
1 1/4 cups chopped carrots
3 garlic cloves, minced
1 tablespoon ground cumin
1 teaspoon salt
2 teaspoons liquid smoke
  flavoring
1/4 pound ham, all fat trimmed,
  cut into 1/4-inch cubes

Combine drained beans with the 3 1/2 cups water through ham cubes, cover and cook on high for 30 minutes. Turn to low and cook for 8 to 9 hours or until beans are very tender. * Remove 3 cups of the soup and puree in a food processor. (Or puree in small batches in a blender.) Return puree to the slow cooker and combine.

2 ounces sun-dried tomatoes,
  not oil-packed

Add sun-dried tomatoes and cook on high, covered, for 20 minutes or until tomatoes are tender.

Eliminate ham for a vegetarian bean soup; fat is reduced to 6%, Calories to 191.

9% calories from fat per serving

Yield: 8 (1 1/2-cup) servings
Nutrient content per serving:
Calories: 217   Fat: 2.2 g   Protein: 14.6 g   Carbohydrate: 34.7 g
Sodium: 621.6 mg   Cholesterol: 7.8 mg   Fiber: 12.6 g

Alternate Method: Cover beans with water and soak overnight. Drain. Place beans in a soup pot with water through ham. Add an additional 1 1/2 cups water. Bring to a boil, reduce to a simmer and cook, covered, for 3 hours or until beans are very tender, stirring occasionally. Continue from * above. After adding tomatoes, simmer, covered, an additional 20 minutes or until tomatoes are tender.

Onion Soup

There is really no substitute for browning the onions in a skillet, but the slow cooker and microwave still make this classic soup easier to prepare.

**2 1/2 pounds yellow onions, peeled
  and thinly sliced
2 tablespoons vegetable oil
1 teaspoon sugar
3 (10-ounce) cans beef broth,
  low-sodium
3 cups water
3 bay leaves
3 whole cloves
1/2 teaspoon dried thyme leaves
1/2 teaspoon dried basil leaves
1/2 teaspoon dried oregano leaves
3/4 teaspoon salt
1/2 teaspoon pepper
1 teaspoon Worcestershire sauce
1/2 cup dry vermouth**

**8 teaspoons grated Parmesan
  cheese**

* Spray a large pan with nonstick cooking spray. Add oil and brown onions over low heat for 30 minutes, stirring occasionally, until onions begin to turn color. Add sugar after 10 minutes. Meanwhile, heat broth and water at high setting in the **microwave** for 5 minutes or until hot. Transfer onions, broth mixture and remaining ingredients through vermouth to the **slow cooker**. Cover and cook on low for 7 to 8 hours. ** Remove bay leaves before serving.

Serve in bowls, top with 1 teaspoon grated cheese.

If desired, eliminate vermouth and increase water to 3 1/2 cups.

28% calories from fat per serving

Yield: 8 (1 1/2-cup) servings
Nutrient content per serving:
Calories: 136   Fat: 4.3 g   Protein: 5.0 g   Carbohydrate: 15.7 g
Sodium: 298.2 mg   Cholesterol: 1.3 mg   Fiber: 2.6 g   Alcohol: 2.1 g

Alternate Method: After browning onions as * above, transfer all ingredients through vermouth to a soup pot. Bring to a boil, reduce heat, and simmer, covered, for 2 hours at a very low temperature. Stir periodically. Continue from ** above.

Lentil Soup with Brown Rice, Roasted Red Peppers and Mushrooms

The roasted red peppers add a unique flavor to this delightful soup.

1 cup brown lentils
3/4 cup brown rice
1 (12-ounce) jar roasted red peppers, drained and chopped into 1-inch pieces
1 pound mushrooms, sliced or quartered
1 (14 1/2-ounce) can chopped tomatoes
1 1/2 cups onion, coarsely chopped
6 cups water
1 teaspoon dried basil leaves
1 teaspoon dried thyme leaves
1 bay leaf
1 teaspoon salt

Combine lentils through salt in a **slow cooker**. Cook at high temperature for 5 hours or until lentils and rice are tender. Remove bay leaf before serving.

4% calories from fat per serving

Yield: 8 (1-cup) servings

Nutrient content per serving:
Calories: 201   Fat: 1.0 g   Protein: 10.2 g   Carbohydrate: 37.7 g
Sodium: 497.2 mg   Cholesterol: 0.0 mg   Fiber: 9.1 g

Alternate Method: Combine all ingredients in a large soup pot. Bring to a boil, reduce to a simmer, cover and cook for 1 hour or until lentils and rice are tender. Stir occasionally.

Vegetarian Chili

Spicy, light, lowfat; what a combination!

1 pound fresh mushrooms,
  quartered
1 green pepper, chopped
  coarsely
1 red pepper, chopped coarsely
1 onion, chopped
3 stalks celery, chopped
2 garlic cloves, minced
2 tablespoons chili powder
2 teaspoons ground cumin
1 (14 1/2-ounce) can chopped
  tomatoes
1 (8-ounce) can tomato sauce
2 teaspoons sugar
1 teaspoon salt
1/8 teaspoon pepper

Combine mushrooms through pepper in a **slow cooker**. Cook on low for 8 hours. If possible, stir after 4 hours.
* Process in a food processor to "chunky" consistency. (Or puree small batches in a blender.) Return to slow cooker.

2 (1-pound) cans low-sodium kidney
  beans, drained

Add beans, combine and heat until warmed, about 15 minutes at high setting.

7% calories from fat per serving

Yield: 8 (1 1/2-cup) servings
Nutrient content per serving:
Calories: 188   Fat: 1.4 g   Protein: 10.0 g   Carbohydrate: 33.8 g
Sodium: 586.0 mg   Cholesterol: 0.0 mg   Fiber: 9.4 g

Alternate Method: Combine all ingredients through pepper in a large soup pot. Bring to a boil, reduce to a simmer, cover and cook for about 1 hour or until vegetables are very tender, stirring occasionally. Continue from * above, but return to soup pot, add beans and heat.

Hearty Vegetable Stew

A meal in itself. Serve with fresh bread for a healthy, low-fat dinner.

1/2 pound frozen "vegetables for stew"
1/2 pound frozen blackeye peas
1/2 pound frozen chopped mustard greens
1/2 pound frozen corn
1 small (6-ounce) zucchini squash, quartered lengthwise and then cut into 1-inch pieces
1 small (6-ounce) yellow squash, quartered lengthwise and then cut into 1-inch pieces
1 1/4 cups chicken broth, defatted
2 tablespoons lemon juice
2 garlic cloves, minced
3/4 teaspoon dried dill weed
1/2 teaspoon salt
1/4 teaspoon pepper

Combine all ingredients in a **slow cooker**. Cook at low temperature for 6 hours. Stir once or twice if possible.

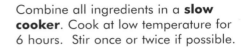

2% calories from fat per serving

Yield: 6 (1-cup) servings
Nutrient content per serving:
Calories: 131   Fat: 0.3 g   Protein: 7.5 g   Carbohydrate: 24.5 g
Sodium: 228.9 mg   Cholesterol: 0.0 mg   Fiber: 3.0 g

Alternate Method: Combine all ingredients in a large soup pot. Bring to a boil, reduce to a simmer and then cook covered for 30 to 35 minutes until vegetables are tender, stirring occasionally.

Black Bean Soup

A 1-pound can of tomatoes, drained, may replace the roasted red pepper if you wish; but the peppers are something special.

3 (15-ounce) cans black beans, drained and rinsed
1 1/2 cups chopped onions
2 garlic cloves, minced
1 (12-ounce) jar roasted red peppers, drained and chopped coarsely
2 1/2 cups low-sodium chicken broth
1 teaspoon chili powder
1/2 teaspoon dried coriander leaves
1 teaspoon ground cumin
1 teaspoon dried oregano leaves
1/4 teaspoon pepper

Combine the onion and garlic cloves with 1/4 cup of the chicken broth in a 3 quart **microwave**-safe casserole. Cover. Cook at high temperature for 5 minutes to soften, stirring after 3 minutes. Add remaining ingredients. Cover and cook at high temperature for 10 minutes. Stir. Cook at medium (50%) setting for 10 minutes more. (Rotate casserole 1/2 turn halfway through both 10 minute cooking periods if microwave does not have a carousel.) Puree slightly in a food processor, if desired. (Or puree in small batches in a blender.)

No additional salt has been added due to high sodium content of canned beans. If desired, season to taste, carefully, and top with a spoonful of nonfat yogurt or fat-free sour cream.

12% calories from fat per serving

Yield: 10 (1-cup) servings

Nutrient content per serving:
Calories: 141   Fat: 1.8 g   Protein: 8.3 g   Carbohydrate: 22.8 g
Sodium: 502.1 mg   Cholesterol: 0.0 mg   Fiber: 8.0 g

Alternate Method: Spray a soup pot with nonstick cooking spray. Saute onions and garlic until softened. Add remaining ingredients, bring to a boil, reduce to a simmer, cover and cook for 30 to 45 minutes, stirring occasionally. Puree slightly, if desired.

Spicy Chili with Beans

No one will believe you didn't slave over the stove for hours preparing this tasty chili.

1/2 pound ground top round
1/2 pound fresh ground turkey breast
1 cup onion, finely chopped
1 (10 1/2-ounce) can beef broth, defatted
1 (8-ounce) can tomato sauce
1/2 teaspoon garlic powder
1 1/2 teaspoons paprika
1 tablespoon ground cumin
1 teaspoon dried oregano leaves
3 tablespoons chili powder
2 (1-pound) cans chili beans, not drained

Place meat in a **microwave**-safe casserole. Cook at high temperature for 4 minutes or until meat is not pink, stirring after 2 minutes to crumble. Add onions and cook 2 minutes more. Break up meat with a wooden spoon to thoroughly crumble. Add ingredients up to chili beans and combine. Cover and cook on high for 6 to 8 minutes or until mixture comes to a simmer. Stir. Cook at medium low (30%), covered, for 25 minutes. Add beans and continue to cook at medium low for 10 minutes more. (Rotate casserole 1/2 turn halfway through each cooking period if microwave does not have a carousel.)

Serve over pasta for a wonderful chili mac dinner. To reduce fat content even further, use one pound fresh ground turkey breast and eliminate the ground round.

14% calories from fat per serving

Yield: 8 (1-cup) servings
Nutrient content per serving:
Calories: 233   Fat: 3.6 g   Protein: 26.2 g   Carbohydrate: 23.9 g
Sodium: 783.0 mg   Cholesterol: 49.9 mg   Fiber: 7.4 g

Alternate Method: Spray a large nonstick skillet well with nonstick cooking spray. Brown meat at low heat, stirring to prevent sticking. Add onions and cook until translucent. Add ingredients through chili powder, cover and cook at very low heat for 1 hour, stirring occasionally. Add beans and continue to cook, covered, for 15 minutes more.

Lentil Soup With Orzo

High in fiber, low in fat, this tasty soup cooks and stays warm in the same serving pot.

1 cup onion, chopped coarsely
1/2 cup carrots, peeled and chopped
1/2 cup celery, chopped
1 garlic clove, minced
1/4 cup fresh parsley, chopped
1 cup brown lentils
3 cups low-sodium vegetable juice
4 cups water
1/2 teaspoon dried basil leaves
1/2 teaspoon dried oregano leaves
3/4 teaspoon salt

Spray **rice cooker** bowl with nonstick cooking spray. Add onion through salt and cook for about 35 minutes.

2 cups low-sodium vegetable juice
1/2 cup orzo (rice-shaped) pasta

Place remaining juice in a **microwave**-safe measuring cup or bowl and cook on high for about 2 1/2 minutes or until it just comes to a simmer. Add heated juice to the rice cooker along with the pasta and cook, covered, for another 20 minutes or until pasta is tender, stirring occasionally.

3% calories from fat per serving

Yield: 6 (1 1/2-cup) servings
Nutrient content per serving:
Calories: 222   Fat: 0.7 g   Protein: 12.6 g   Carbohydrate: 43.1 g
Sodium: 372.4 mg   Cholesterol: 0.0 mg   Fiber: 11.6 g

Alternate Method: Spray a soup pot with nonstick cooking spray. Add onion through salt, bring to a boil, reduce heat, cover and simmer for 35 minutes. Add remaining juice, return to a simmer, add pasta, cover and cook for another 20 minutes or until pasta is tender, stirring occasionally.

Giant White Beans With Potatoes and Shell Pasta

This is a delightful soup. The slow cooker is excellent when used to cook dried beans.

1 cup dried giant white beans

Soak beans in water to cover overnight. Drain.

2 stalks celery, chopped
1 cup onion, chopped
1/2 cup carrots, chopped
1 1/2 cups potato, peeled and cut into 1/2-inch pieces
2 garlic cloves, minced
2 (10-ounce) cans beef broth, defatted
1 (14 1/2-ounce) can diced tomatoes
1 cup water
1 teaspoon dried coriander leaves
1 teaspoon dried thyme leaves

Place beans in the **slow cooker** along with celery through thyme. Cook on high temperature for 5 to 6 hours or until beans are tender, but not mushy.
* Remove 1 cup bean and vegetable mixture and puree in a food processor or a blender.

1 cup small shell pasta

Return to the slow cooker along with pasta and cook on high for 30 to 40 minutes or until pasta is just tender. Add a little hot water if a thinner soup is desired.

Imported pasta produces a better result in a slow cooker. Generally, the durum wheat is "harder", so the pasta is not "mushy".

5% calories from fat per serving

Yield: 6 (1 1/2-cup) servings
Nutrient content per serving:
Calories: 270   Fat: 1.4 g   Protein: 11.4 g   Carbohydrate: 53.0 g
Sodium: 461.6 mg   Cholesterol: 0.9 mg   Fiber: 8.8 g

Alternate Method: Place drained soaked beans in a soup pot. Add celery through thyme and bring to a boil, reduce to a simmer, cover and cook for about 1 1/2 hours or until beans are tender, but not mushy. Puree and return to pot as * above. Add pasta and cook for 10 minutes or until it is just tender.

Savory Zucchini Soup

Easy, pretty, tasty...this soup has it all! Serve from the cooking casserole.

2 pounds (about 6 medium) zucchini squash, scrubbed, cut into 1-inch pieces
1 1/2 cups onion, coarsely chopped
1 cup chicken broth, defatted
1/4 cup fresh chopped parsley
1 teaspoon dried thyme leaves
1/2 teaspoon celery seed
1 teaspoon salt

Combine squash through salt in a 3-quart **microwave**-safe casserole. Cover. Cook at high for 12-15 minutes or until squash is very tender. (Rotate casserole 1/2 turn halfway through cooking time if microwave does not have a carousel.) Rest for 5 minutes.

2 tablespoons flour

Add flour to squash mixture and puree in a food processor. Return mixture to the casserole.

1 cup skim milk

Add milk and combine. Cover. Microwave at high for 5 minutes, whisking after every minute or until soup is slightly thickened.

This soup is good warm or cold.

4% calories from fat per serving

Yield: 6 (1-cup) servings
Nutrient content per serving:
Calories: 71   Fat: 0.3 g   Protein: 4.1 g   Carbohydrate: 12.9 g
Sodium: 417.8 mg   Cholesterol: 0.7 mg   Fiber: 0.9 g

Alternate Method: Combine squash through salt in a saucepan. Bring to a boil, reduce heat, cover and simmer for 15 to 20 minutes or until squash is tender. Add flour and puree. Return mixture to the saucepan, add milk and simmer for 5 to 10 minutes or until soup is slightly thickened, stirring frequently.

Curried Carrot Soup

Use pre-packaged peeled baby carrots to save time putting together this easy nutritious soup. It's very high in vitamin A (2393 RE/serving) and Beta carotene (2407 Ug/serving).

3 cups carrots, peeled and chopped into pieces no greater than 1 inch
1 cup onion, coarsely chopped
2 cups chicken broth, defatted, divided
3/4 teaspoon curry powder
1 teaspoon salt
1/8 teaspoon white pepper

Combine carrots, onion and 1 cup broth in a 3-quart, **microwave**-safe casserole. Cover. Cook in the microwave at high temperature for 15 minutes or until carrots are very tender. (Rotate casserole 1/2 turn halfway through cooking time if microwave does not have a carousel.) Rest 5 minutes. Puree mixture in a food processor. (Or puree small batches in a blender.) Return puree to the casserole and add remaining broth and seasonings. Cover. Cook at high temperature for 3 to 5 minutes or until mixture just comes to a simmer.

1 cup plain nonfat yogurt, strained for 25 minutes (see Yogurt Cheese, page 235)
1 tablespoon fresh chives

* Whisk in strained yogurt a little at a time. Top with chives.

Good warm or cold. Do not reheat after yogurt has been added as yogurt may separate and appear "curdled".

3% calories from fat per serving

Yield: 6 (1-cup) servings
Nutrient content per serving:
Calories: 92   Fat: 0.3 g   Protein: 5.6 g   Carbohydrate: 16.8 g
Sodium: 462.8 mg   Cholesterol: 1.7 mg   Fiber: 3.1 g

Alternate Method: Combine carrots, onion and 1 cup broth in a saucepan, bring to a boil, reduce to a simmer, cover and cook about 15 minutes or until vegetables are tender. Puree. Return puree to the pan and add remaining broth and seasonings. Heat at low temperature just until it comes to a simmer. Turn off heat. Continue from * above.

Main Dishes

Main Dishes
Poultry

Notes

Chicken Strips and Rice

Walk away after you turn on the rice cooker; come back in 20 minutes to a nutritious, low-fat meal.

1 tablespoon olive oil
1 cup long-grain white rice
2 pounds chicken breast, skinned,
**   boned, cut into 1-inch strips**
3 cups chicken broth, defatted
1 teaspoon dried thyme leaves
3/4 teaspoon paprika
1/2 teaspoon salt
1/8 teaspoon black pepper

Combine rice and oil in a **microwave**-safe bowl. Cover. Microwave at high temperature for about 6 minutes, stirring every minute until lightly browned. Spray **rice cooker** bowl with nonstick cooking spray and combine browned rice with remaining ingredients. Turn on rice cooker and cook for 20 to 25 minutes or until broth is nearly absorbed. Turn machine off and/or unplug. Let mixture sit for 5 minutes. Toss gently.

18% calories from fat per serving

Yield: 6 servings
Nutrient content per serving:
Calories: 363   Fat: 7.1 g   Protein: 49.1 g   Carbohydrate: 25.0 g
Sodium: 299.5 mg   Cholesterol: 116.2 mg   Fiber: 0.5 g

Alternate Method: In a heavy, 3-quart pan, brown rice in heated oil for 5 to 10 minutes, or until lightly browned, stirring frequently. Turn off heat and CAREFULLY add remaining ingredients (reduce broth to 2 1/2 cups). Bring to a boil, reduce heat and simmer for 20 to 25 minutes, covered, or until broth is nearly absorbed. Let mixture sit for 5 minutes. Toss gently.

Roast Chicken with Stuffing

Ignore this chicken and you'll still produce an elegant meal! This is a low-fat version of the well-known use for the heatproof oven bag. There will be no cleanup and no basting.

flour
1 (3-pound) roaster chicken,
    washed, dried and trimmed
    of excess fat
1 teaspoon vegetable oil
1 teaspoon poultry seasoning
1/8 teaspoon pepper
1 (6-ounce) box stuffing mix
    with herbs
1 tablespoon margarine
white twine
poultry pin

Preheat oven to 325 degrees. Add the amount of flour to **heatproof oven bag** according to package directions. * Rub the chicken with oil, poultry seasoning and pepper. Make the stuffing according to package directions, except use 1 tablespoon margarine instead of directed amount. Stuff chicken cavity with about 1 1/2 cups of the stuffing, and place the rest in a small heatsafe bowl. (Bake along with chicken for the last 30 minutes.) Pin chicken cavity closed and tie the legs with twine. Place the chicken in the oven bag in a baking pan. Tie and vent according to package directions. Bake for about 1 1/2 to 2 hours or until the temperature is 185 degrees. ** Test the inside of a thigh at the thickest part with an instant-read thermometer. (Insert through the oven bag.) Chicken should be nicely browned and the legs should move easily in the sockets. Remove the chicken from the oven bag and skim all fat from the juices with a gravy skimmer. Remove the stuffing from the cavity and discard the skin. Cut the chicken into serving pieces and serve with the defatted juices. (If no stuffing is desired, stuff with an onion and a celery stalk, halved, and reduce cooking time by 15 minutes.)

For later eating, freeze the chicken in its oven bag. Refer to "Storage Uses of the Heatproof Oven Bag" on page 231 for details. Couldn't be easier or more convenient. The nutrition numbers assume that you eat an equal amount of light and dark meat!

31% calories from fat per serving

Yield: 4 servings

Nutrient content per serving:

Calories: 427   Fat: 14.5 g   Protein: 41.1 g   Carbohydrate: 32.9 g
Sodium: 955.7 mg   Cholesterol: 108.5 mg   Fiber: 0.1 g

Alternate Method: Preheat oven to 350 degrees. Spray a roasting pan with nonstick cooking spray. Prepare the chicken and stuffing as * above. Place chicken in the pan, breast down, and bake for 1 1/2 to 2 hours basting frequently with pan juices until temperature is 185 degrees. Turn chicken carefully halfway through cooking time so breast is up. Continue from ** above.

Chicken Breast Packages In Curry Marinade

Chicken breasts in packages are so very moist and tender. Marinate and assemble in advance and cook at the last minute.

1/4 cup tomato sauce
1/3 cup white wine
2 teaspoons vegetable oil
1 tablespoon sugar
1 teaspoon curry powder
1 teaspoon Worcestershire sauce
1/2 teaspoon salt
1 garlic clove, minced
3 dashes hot pepper sauce
4 (4-ounce) chicken breasts, boned, skinned, all fat removed

* Combine tomato sauce through pepper sauce in a zip-top heavy-duty plastic storage bag. Place chicken breasts in the marinade, seal, and turn bag to coat chicken. Refrigerate for at least 2 hours. Cut 4 pieces of heavy-duty foil 12 inches long. Remove chicken from marinade, place on the foil, and seal edges. Reserve marinade. **Grill** on medium high heat for 5 minutes on each side. Rest 10 minutes before opening packages. Meat should be springy to the touch. Simmer reserved marinade for about 3 minutes and serve with the chicken.

This recipe can be prepared in the microwave using directions for "Chicken Packages With Salsa", page 81.

27% calories from fat per serving

Yield: 4 servings
Nutrient content per serving:
Calories: 178   Fat: 5.4 g   Protein: 27.1 g   Carbohydrate: 5.2 g
Sodium: 460.7 mg   Cholesterol: 73.0 mg   Fiber: 0.4 g

Alternate Method: Marinate breasts as * above. Remove them and place in a baking pan large enough to hold them in one layer, reserving marinade. Bake in a preheated 350 degree oven for about 30 minutes or until they are springy to the touch and juices run clear. Baste frequently with reserved marinade. Simmer marinade about 3 minutes and serve with the chicken.

Roasted Chicken Breasts With Garlic

Leave the skin on the breasts while cooking for a juicy result; but don't cheat - remove the skin before serving!

flour
4 large chicken breasts, bone-in, skin-on (about 8 ounces each)
4 garlic cloves, halved lengthwise
1 teaspoon dried oregano leaves
1/4 teaspoon salt

Preheat oven to 325 degrees. Add the amount of flour to **heatproof oven bag** according to package directions. * Loosen skin from each breast, but do not remove completely. Sprinkle oregano and salt directly onto breast meat, lay 2 halves of garlic on each breast then pull skin back over to cover. Place breasts in the oven bag. Tie and vent according to package directions and place the oven bag in a baking pan. Bake for 45 minutes to 1 hour or until a sharp knife slices meat easily and juices run clear. Skin should be lightly browned and bubbly. Do not overbake. (Test meat by cutting through the oven bag.) Remove skin before serving.

Great with spicy tomato salsa on the side.

20% calories from fat per serving

Yield: 4 servings
Nutrient content per serving:
Calories: 275   Fat: 6.2 g   Protein: 53.6 g   Carbohydrate: 1.2 g
Sodium: 273.0 mg   Cholesterol: 146 mg   Fiber: 0.1 g

Alternate Method: Prepare breasts as * above but place directly in a baking pan. Pour 1/2 cup chicken broth, defatted, around the breasts. Cover. Bake in a preheated 350 degree oven, basting frequently with broth, for about 1 hour. Uncover the last 15 minutes. Remove skin before serving.

Chicken Breasts with Mint and Honey

Marinate and bake in the same heatproof oven bag with no cleanup afterwards. Hallelujah!

flour
2 tablespoons honey
2 tablespoons Dijon mustard
1 tablespoon red or white wine vinegar
1 tablespoon vegetable oil
1 teaspoon dried mint leaves
1/4 teaspoon salt
dash pepper
4 (5-ounce) chicken breasts, skinned, bone-in

Preheat oven to 325 degrees. Add the amount of flour to **heatproof oven bag** according to package directions. Combine honey through pepper in the oven bag and squeeze to combine. Place chicken breasts in the oven bag and turn so marinade coats chicken pieces. Tie. Marinate, refrigerated, at least two hours. Vent according to package directions and place the oven bag in a baking pan, making sure that chicken pieces are in one layer and bone side is down. Bake for 30 to 40 minutes or until * a sharp knife slices meat easily and juices run clear. (Test meat by cutting through the oven bag.) Serve with juices.

26% calories from fat per serving

Yield: 4 servings
Nutrient content per serving:
Calories: 345   Fat: 10.1 g   Protein: 53.9 g   Carbohydrate: 9.5 g
Sodium: 315.6 mg   Cholesterol: 146.2 mg   Fiber: 0.2 g

Alternate Method: Combine honey through pepper in a heavy duty zip-top plastic storage bag. Add chicken and marinate, refrigerated, for at least 2 hours. Preheat oven to 350 degrees. Transfer chicken from the storage bag to a baking pan, bone side up, reserving the marinade. Bake, covered, for 25 minutes. Turn chicken over, baste with the reserved marinade, and bake, uncovered, for an additional 10 minutes or until the chicken tests done as * above.

Chicken Packages with Salsa

The microwave can produce a wonderfully juicy chicken breast, especially in packages. Caution: don't overcook!

6 (4-ounce) chicken breasts, skinned, boned and all fat removed
3/4 cup commercial salsa
6 green onions, cleaned, trimmed and halved

Cut 12 pieces of waxed paper 14 inches long and use two at a time. Place one chicken breast on the paper, spread with 1 tablespoon salsa and top with 2 green onion halves. Seal as if closing a package and place, folded side under and onion up, in a **microwave**-safe plate large enough to hold the packages in one layer. (Refrigerate, if desired, up to a day in advance. Bring to room temperature before cooking.) Microwave at high temperature for 3 minutes. Turn each package over. (Rotate 1/2 turn if microwave does not have a carousel.) Microwave 3 minutes more. Rest 5 minutes. * Chicken tests done when a finger pressed in the chicken does not leave an indentation. Unwrap packages carefully and serve with juices.

1/2 cup commercial salsa

Pass additional salsa, if desired.

18% calories from fat per serving

Yield: 6 servings
Nutrient content per serving:
Calories: 157   Fat: 3.1 g   Protein: 26.8 g   Carbohydrate: 5.4 g
Sodium: 197.1 mg   Cholesterol: 73.0 mg   Fiber: 1.8 g

Alternate Method: Preheat oven to 350 degrees. Place chicken in one layer in a flat, glass or ceramic, casserole. Pour 3/4 cup salsa over chicken. Top with onion. Bake for about 30 minutes, basting with salsa, or until chicken tests done as * above.

Quick Barbeque Chicken

A speedy, easy way to grill unboned chicken.

6 (6-ounce) chicken breasts,
   bone-in and skin-on
1 cup commercial barbeque sauce

Place chicken in one layer in a **microwave**-safe casserole. Cover. Cook at high for 3 to 4 minutes per pound total weight. Drain liquid. Brush with barbeque sauce. Spray the **grill** with nonstick cooking spray. Grill chicken at medium high heat until it is just browned, about 3 to 5 minutes on each side. * Remove the skin and brush chicken with additional sauce.

Prepare in advance and refrigerate or freeze in a heatproof oven bag. Refer to "Storage Uses of the Heatproof Oven Bag" on page 231 for details.

16% calories from fat per serving

Yield: 6 servings

Nutrient content per serving:

Calories: 338   Fat: 6.1 g   Protein: 53.4 g   Carbohydrate: 17.3 g
Sodium: 500.3 mg   Cholesterol: 146.0 mg   Fiber: 0.7 g

Alternate Method: Spray a broiler pan with nonstick cooking spray. Brush chicken with barbeque sauce. Broil under medium broiler about 5 to 6 inches from the heat for a total of 30 minutes turning and basting after 15 minutes. Watch so it doesn't burn. Continue from * above.

Lemon Chicken

Couldn't be easier to prepare a tender, juicy, whole chicken.

1 (3-pound) roaster chicken, washed, dried and trimmed of excess fat
1 lemon, washed
2/3 cup chicken broth, defatted
2 tablespoons (1/2 package) dry onion soup mix

* Remove a 4-inch strip of zest from the lemon (only the colored part) with a vegetable peeler. Halve the lemon and squeeze juice over the chicken. Place the zest in the chicken cavity. Place chicken in the **slow cooker** and pour some of the broth over it to moisten. Rub all over with dry onion soup. Pour remaining broth around the chicken. Cover. Cook at low temperature for about 8 hours or until chicken is very tender. ** Lift it out carefully, remove the skin, and cut it into serving pieces. Remove all fat from the juices with a gravy skimmer and serve the juices with the chicken.

For later eating, freeze the chicken in a heatproof oven bag. Refer to "Storage Uses of the Heatproof Oven Bag" on page 231 for details. The nutrition numbers assume that you eat an equal amount of light and dark meat!

33% calories from fat per serving

Yield: 4 servings
Nutrient content per serving:
Calories: 258   Fat: 9.4 g   Protein: 37.8 g   Carbohydrate: 5.5 g
Sodium: 546.6 mg   Cholesterol: 108.7 mg   Fiber: 0.5 g

Alternate Method: Preheat oven to 350 degrees. Spray a baking pan with nonstick cooking spray. Prepare the chicken from * above. Place chicken in the baking pan and roast for about 1 1/2 hours, basting frequently with pan juices. Continue from ** above.

Red Beans and Sausage Over Rice

Dried beans are so easy to prepare in the slow cooker - no stirring, no watching. Use smoked salt flavoring instead of the traditional salt pork. Fat-free turkey sausage will reduce the fat percentage to only 2%!

1 pound dried, red kidney beans
6 cups water

Place dried beans and water in the **slow cooker**. Cover and cook at low temperature (overnight) for 8 to 10 hours until they are just tender but not mushy. Drain and return to the slow cooker.

2 cups onion, chopped
3 garlic cloves, minced
2 celery stalks, chopped
1 (10-ounce) can low-sodium beef broth
1 1/4 cups water
2 bay leaves
1/4 teaspoon smoked salt flavoring
2 teaspoons dried thyme leaves
1 teaspoon dried oregano leaves
1/2 teaspoon hot pepper sauce

Add onion through pepper sauce. Cover and cook at low temperature for 8 hours. Remove bay leaves.

1 pound turkey sausage, cut into 1/2-inch slices

Remove and puree 1 1/2 cups beans and return to the cooker along with sausage. Cook at high temperature for 30 minutes or until sausage is heated.

6 cups cooked white rice

For each serving, place about 3/4 cup rice on a plate and top with 1 cup bean mixture.

Pass the hot sauce if you like beans "flaming".

12% calories from fat per serving

Yield: 8 servings

Nutrient content per serving:

Calories: 458   Fat: 6.0 g   Protein: 27.1 g   Carbohydrate: 73.9 g

Sodium: 584.7 mg   Cholesterol: 35.4 mg   Fiber: 15.6 g

Alternate Method: Soak beans in water for at least 8 hours. Drain. In a large soup pot, combine beans through pepper sauce, bring to a boil, reduce to a simmer, cover and cook for about 2 hours. Stir periodically. Add more water if mixture becomes too thick. Remove and puree 1 1/2 cups beans. Return pureed beans to the pot with the sausage and cook for another 30 minutes. Serve over rice.

Simple Grilled Marinated Chicken Breasts

Marinate breasts in Klestene's Dressing (page 202) for a zesty flavor; but fat percentage will be 32%.

6 (4-ounce) chicken breasts, boned, skinned
1 1/4 cups commercial fat-free Italian dressing (reserve 1/4 cup)
1 teaspoon vegetable oil

* Combine 1 cup dressing with oil in a heavy-duty zip-top plastic storage bag or a glass bowl. Add breasts to the dressing and marinate, refrigerated, for at least 2 hours, but not more than 8 hours. Turn at least twice during this period. Spray **grill** with nonstick cooking spray. Remove chicken from marinade and grill for 4 to 5 minutes on each side, depending on the thickness, at medium heat. Brush with marinade at least once on each side. Chicken is done when it does not leave an indentation when touched lightly with a finger. Do not overcook. Cool slightly and cut diagonally into 3/4-inch slices. Toss with reserved 1/4 cup dressing and serve over salad or pasta.

A slight amount of oil added to commercial fat-free dressing produces a better grilled chicken breast.

23% calories from fat per serving

Yield: 6 servings
Nutrient content per serving:
Calories: 152   Fat: 3.8 g   Protein: 26.7 g   Carbohydrate: 2.7 g
Sodium: 449.7 mg   Cholesterol: 73 mg   Fiber: 0.0 g

Alternate Method: Marinate chicken as * above. Spray a broiler pan with nonstick cooking spray. Remove chicken from marinade and broil under medium broiler 5 to 6 inches from the heat, for about 5 minutes on each side. Baste at least once on each side. Watch carefully to avoid overcooking.

Easy Paella

A mock version of the famous Spanish dish. Use turmeric powder instead of saffron for economy; but expect the taste to be different.

2 (4-ounce) chicken breast halves, skinned, boned, cut into 1-inch pieces
6 ounces smoked turkey sausage, fully cooked, sliced into 1/2-inch pieces
1 cup long-grain white rice
2 2/3 cups chicken broth, defatted
1 cup onion, chopped
1 green pepper, washed and cored, cut into 1-inch pieces
1/4 cup fresh parsley or 1 tablespoon, dried
1 teaspoon dried oregano leaves
1/8 teaspoon pepper
large pinch saffron
6 ounces frozen, cooked shrimp, prepared according to package directions

Spray the **rice cooker** container with nonstick cooking spray. Combine all ingredients except shrimp in the cooker. Turn on the machine. Add shrimp after about 30 minutes. (Do not combine, let shrimp sit on top of the other ingredients.) Cook for about 10 minutes longer or until broth is nearly absorbed. Turn machine off and/or unplug. * Let the mixture sit for 5 minutes. Remaining broth will be absorbed. Toss gently.

13% calories from fat per serving

Yield: 6 servings
Nutrient content per serving:
Calories: 254   Fat: 3.8 g   Protein: 23.7 g   Carbohydrate: 31.3 g
Sodium: 479.2 mg   Cholesterol: 83.7 mg   Fiber: 1.7 g

Alternate Method: Spray a saucepan with nonstick cooking spray. Combine ingredients as above, bring to boil, cover and simmer for 15 minutes. Add shrimp and simmer, covered, for about 10 minutes longer or until broth is nearly absorbed. Continue from * above.

Braised Turkey Breast with Onions

Probably the easiest turkey you'll ever prepare. The slow cooker produces a wonderfully moist and tender meat.

1/2 teaspoon salt
1/8 teaspoon pepper
1 teaspoon dried thyme leaves
1 (3-pound) turkey breast half,
skinned
2 large white onions, each cut into
1/6ths
1 1/4 cups canned chicken broth,
defatted

* Combine salt, pepper and thyme. Rub mixture over meat side of turkey breast. Place turkey in the **slow cooker**, bone side up. Surround with onions. Pour broth over onions. Cook on high temperature for 30 minutes, then reduce temperature to low and cook for 8 to 9 hours or until turkey is very tender. ** Remove turkey. Remove all fat from the remaining juices with a gravy skimmer. Let turkey stand for 15 minutes, covered loosely, before carving. Surround with onions. Pour a little of the juices over the turkey and onions and pass the rest.

7% calories from fat per serving

Yield: 8 servings
Nutrient content per serving:
Calories: 246   Fat: 2 g   Protein: 53 g   Carbohydrate: 4 g
Sodium: 477 mg   Cholesterol: 141 mg   Fiber: 0.8 g

Alternate Method: Prepare meat as * above and place the turkey, breast side up, in a Dutch oven. Surround with onions and add broth. Bring it to a boil, reduce to a simmer, cover and braise in a preheated 325 degree oven for about 2 hours or until an instant-read thermometer registers 170 degrees. Baste occasionally. Continue from ** above.

Grilled Turkey Patties "Surprise"

The potato gives the turkey patties a wonderful light texture, the chilies liven up the taste.

1 pound fresh ground turkey breast
1/2 pound russet potato
1/4 cup skim milk
1 egg white
1/2 teaspoon onion powder
1/2 teaspoon garlic powder
1/2 teaspoon salt
1/4 teaspoon white pepper

Pierce potato with a fork. **Microwave** at high temperature for about 4 minutes or until done. * Cool. Peel. Chop coarsely. Process along with turkey through pepper in a food processor until well combined.

6 tablespoons chopped green chilies

Turn mixture into a bowl and add chilies by hand. (Mixture will be sticky.) Form into 8 patties. Spray **grill** with nonstick cooking spray. Grill patties for 5 minutes on each side at medium heat spraying patties with nonstick cooking spray before turning.

1/2 cup commercial chunky salsa

Serve with salsa if desired.

Olives or sun dried tomatoes are also tasty in these patties.

6% calories from fat per serving

Yield: 8 servings

Nutrient content per serving:
Calories: 112   Fat: 0.7 g   Protein: 18.6 g   Carbohydrate: 7.9 g
Sodium: 342.7 mg   Cholesterol: 48.9 mg   Fiber: 0.6 g

Alternate Method: Bake potato in a 425 preheated oven for 50 to 60 minutes. Combine ingredients and form into patties as * above. Spray a broiler pan with nonstick cooking spray. Broil patties 5 to 6 inches from heat in a preheated broiler for about 5 minutes on each side. Spray patties when turning and serve with salsa, if desired.

Turkey Sausage With Red Beans and Brown Rice

You're twenty minutes away from a delicious, nutritious meal. Fat-free turkey sausage will reduce the amount of fat per serving to, yes it's true, only 3% (1 gram)!

1 (16-ounce) can stewed tomatoes
1/2 cup onion, chopped
1 pound fully cooked turkey
**   sausage, cut into 1/2-inch pieces**
1 (16-ounce) can kidney beans,
**   drained and rinsed**
1 cup instant brown rice
1 teaspoon ground cumin
1 teaspoon dried oregano leaves
1/4 teaspoon garlic powder
1/4 teaspoon salt

Drain tomatoes and add water to drained liquid to measure 1 1/2 cups. Soften onions by placing them in 1/4 cup water in a small **microwave**-safe dish. Cover. Microwave at high temperature for 2 minutes. Drain. Spray **rice cooker** container with nonstick cooking spray. Combine liquid and remaining ingredients through salt in the rice cooker. Cook for 16 to 18 minutes or until liquid is nearly absorbed. Turn machine off and/or unplug. * Stir. Let sit at least 5 minutes.

6 tablespoons salsa

Top each serving with 1 tablespoon salsa.

24% calories from fat per serving

Yield: 6 servings
Nutrient content per serving:
Calories: 289   Fat: 7.7 g   Protein: 18.6 g   Carbohydrate: 36.3 g
Sodium: 968.5 mg   Cholesterol: 52.4 mg   Fiber: 52.4 g

Alternate Method: Drain tomatoes and add water to drained liquid to measure 1 cup. Spray a saucepan with nonstick cooking spray. Add onions and soften by cooking at a low temperature, stirring, for a couple of minutes. Add liquid and remaining ingredients through salt. Bring mixture to a boil, reduce to a simmer, and cook, covered, for about 10 minutes or until liquid is nearly absorbed. Continue from * above.

Grilled Turkey Fillets with Cranberry Marinade

Tired of carving the turkey? This might be the beginning of a whole new tradition.

6 (4-ounce) fillets of turkey breast, skinned
3/4 cup canned whole berry cranberry sauce
1/4 cup white wine
1/3 cup apple juice
2 tablespoons lemon juice
1/2 teaspoon poultry seasoning
1/2 teaspoon salt

Place cranberry sauce in a **microwave**-safe bowl. Cover and cook on high for 2 minutes or until it is melted. Add wine through salt and combine. Place fillets in one layer in a heavy-duty zip-top plastic food storage bag. Add 3/4 cup cranberry sauce mixture. Seal the top and turn the bag so the liquid covers all sides of meat. Marinate for at least 2 hours or overnight. Spray a **grill** with nonstick cooking spray. Remove turkey from marinade and grill for 4 to 5 minutes on each side, depending on the thickness, at medium heat. Brush with reserved marinade at least once on each side. Turkey is done when it does not leave an indentation when touched lightly with a finger. Do not overcook. Heat reserved cranberry mixture for about 1 minute on high in microwave and serve with the turkey fillets.

4% calories from fat per serving

Yield: 6 servings
Nutrient content per serving:
Calories: 208   Fat: 0.9 g   Protein: 34.2 g   Carbohydrate: 15.7 g
Sodium: 263.7 mg   Cholesterol: 94.1 mg   Fiber: 0.4 g

Alternate Method: Prepare fillets and grill in a broiler or braise in the cranberry mixture as follows: Combine cranberry sauce through salt in a large skillet. Heat and stir until sauce is melted and ingredients are combined. Add turkey fillets, bring liquid to a simmer, cover and cook for 8 to 10 minutes or until turkey is just done. Remove fillets. (To thicken juices, refer to directions on page 236.) Serve fillets with pan juices.

Turkey Breast in Tomato Sauce

One of the best meats for the slow cooker, the turkey breast is almost a perfect food.

1 (3-pound) turkey breast half, skinned
1 (14 1/2-ounce) can chopped tomatoes
1 onion, sliced
1/4 cup white wine
1 teaspoon dried tarragon leaves
1 teaspoon sugar
1 teaspoon salt
1/8 teaspoon pepper
1/4 teaspoon garlic powder

Place turkey breast in the **slow cooker** bone side up. Combine remaining ingredients and pour over turkey. Cook at high temperature for 30 minutes, then reduce temperature to low and cook for 8 to 9 hours or until turkey is very tender. * Remove turkey. Remove all fat from the remaining juices with a gravy skimmer. (To thicken juices, refer to directions on page 236.) Let turkey stand for 15 minutes, covered loosely, before carving. Pour a little of the juices over the turkey and pass the rest.

Freeze leftovers in a heatproof oven bag. Refer to "Storage Uses of the Heatproof Oven Bag" on page 231 for details.

8% calories from fat per serving

Yield: 8 servings
Nutrient content per serving:
Calories: 241   Fat: 2.1 g   Protein: 51.9 g   Carbohydrate: 3.7 g
Sodium: 400.0 mg   Cholesterol: 146.3 mg   Fiber: 0.7 g

Alternate Method: Place turkey, breast side up, in a Dutch oven. Combine remaining ingredients and pour over turkey. Bring liquid to a boil, reduce to a simmer, cover, and braise in a preheated 325 degree oven for about 2 hours or until an instant-read thermometer registers 170 degrees. Baste occasionally. Continue from * above.

Main Dishes
Beef and Lamb

Old-Fashioned Meat Loaf

Meatloaf in the microwave is not only super-fast, it can also be super-moist! And this one is also super-low-fat.

4 slices white bread, toasted
1 pound lean ground round
1 pound fresh ground turkey breast
2 egg whites
1/3 cup catsup
1 cup onion, chopped
2 teaspoons dried oregano leaves,
   crushed
1/2 teaspoon cinnamon
1 1/2 teaspoons salt
1/4 teaspoon pepper

2 tablespoons catsup

* Soak toast in water and squeeze dry. Combine all ingredients through pepper in a large bowl. Form into a round, doughnut shape in a **microwave**-safe dish, at least 11 inches in diameter. Place a small, microwave-safe glass, upside-down, in the center. (The juices will collect in the glass and it will also help to ensure the even cooking of the meat.)

Brush with additional catsup. Microwave on high, uncovered, for 20 to 25 minutes. (Rotate dish 1/2 turn halfway through cooking time if microwave does not have a carousel.) Let sit for 5 minutes before cutting. ** Internal temperature should be 160 to 170 degrees. If desired, use an instant-read thermometer.

For an even faster assembly, use commercial packaged frozen chopped onions. Microwave on high for 2 minutes. Drain liquid. Proceed with recipe.

12% calories from fat per serving

Yield: 10 servings
Nutrient content per serving:
Calories: 156   Fat: 2.1 g   Protein: 28.0 g   Carbohydrate: 6.3 g
Sodium: 568.8 mg   Cholesterol: 72.7 mg   Fiber: 0.9 g

Alternate Method: Spray a 9x5-inch loaf pan with nonstick cooking spray. Prepare meatloaf as * above, but form into a loaf shape and place in the loaf pan. Baste with catsup and bake in a preheated 350 degree oven for about 1 hour 15 minutes or until it tests done as above **.

London Broil in Soy Marinade

Once upon a time, the cut of beef called "London Broil" meant flank steak. Today, grocers sell various cuts of steak and call them all "London Broil". Top round is the leanest; therefore, it is used here.

cloves, minced

oons low-sodium soy sauce

oons lemon juice

oon vegetable oil

on sugar

, sliced

ound) beef top round

ut 1 1/2 inches thick, all

oved, scored by making

cuts at 1-inch intervals

Combine garlic through sugar in a heavy-duty zip-top plastic storage bag. Add meat and onions and turn so meat is coated with marinade. Seal. Marinate, refrigerated, for 8 hours or overnight. Turn bag a couple of times during this period. Remove meat and onions from marinade and reserve marinade. Spray **grill** with nonstick cooking spray. * Grill meat at medium high temperature for 8 to 10 minutes on each side or until done to taste, basting occasionally with marinade. Let it stand for 10 minutes before cutting. Meanwhile, spray a grill rack with nonstick cooking spray. Grill onion slices on the rack for 2 to 3 minutes, tossing, until just cooked to your taste. ** Slice meat into thin slices, against the grain and toss with the onions.

30% calories from fat per serving

Yield: 6 servings
Nutrient content per serving:

Calories: 267   Fat: 9.1 g   Protein: 37.3 g   Carbohydrate: 9.0 g

Sodium: 273.7 mg   Cholesterol: 95.3 mg   Fiber: 1.5 g

Alternate Method: Spray a broiler pan with nonstick cooking spray. Broil meat 5 to 6 inches from the heat for 8 to 10 minutes on each side as * above. Spray a skillet with the spray and cook onions, stirring constantly, until they are cooked to your taste. Continue from ** above.

Greek Pot Roast

Yiayia's own, loaded with garlic and oregano. But less fat and Calories than Yiayia's! (Who's Yiayia? My Greek grandmother, of course.)

1 teaspoon salt
2 teaspoons dried oregano
  leaves
1 (3-pound) beef top round
  roast, all fat removed
3 garlic cloves, halved
  lengthwise
1 cup beef broth, defatted
2 tablespoons red wine
1 tablespoon tomato paste

* Combine salt and oregano. Make 6 (1/2-inch) slashes in the roast. Into each, insert a piece of garlic and some of the salt-oregano mixture. Rub the roast with the remaining oregano mixture. Place roast in the **slow cooker**. Combine broth through tomato paste. Pour over roast. Cover and cook at low temperature for 8 to 10 hours or until meat is tender and done. For medium well, temperature should be 165 degrees. Use an instant-read thermometer. Remove meat and keep warm.

1 tablespoon beef broth,
  defatted or red wine
1 tablespoon cornstarch

** To thicken juices, combine broth or wine and cornstarch, remove all fat from the juices remaining in the slow cooker with a gravy skimmer, return juices to the slow cooker, whisk in cornstarch mixture and blend well. Cook at high temperature for a few minutes, stirring, until slightly thickened.

Slow cooking requires no browning of the meat due to the low cooking temperature. Less liquid is used since there is virtually no evaporation. Nutrient values are given for ingredients used in the slow cooking recipe.

29% calories from fat per serving

Yield: 12 servings

Nutrient content per serving:

Calories: 212   Fat: 6.8 g   Protein: 36.5 g   Carbohydrate: 1.3 g

Sodium: 291.7 mg   Cholesterol: 95.3 mg   Fiber: 0.1 g

Alternate Method: Prepare meat as * above. Place in a Dutch oven which has been coated with nonstick cooking spray. Brown slowly on all sides. Remove roast from pot. Combine broth through tomato paste (increase broth to 10 ounces, wine to 1/2 cup, tomato paste to 2 tablespoons), and add it to the pan with 3/4 cup water. Bring liquid to a boil, scraping up bits on bottom of the pan. Reduce heat, add meat and simmer, covered, for 1 1/2 to 2 hours or until meat is tender and tests about 165 degrees for medium well. Turn meat periodically while cooking to keep moistened. Thicken juices as ** above doubling amounts of cornstarch and broth or wine.

Beef Stroganoff

An old favorite, revived, easier and lighter than ever.

1 (1 1/2-pound) lean, boneless, top round steak, cut into 1/4-inch by 2-inch strips
1 teaspoon salt
1/4 teaspoon pepper
1 teaspoon dried thyme leaves
3 tablespoons flour
1 cup beef broth, defatted
1 tablespoon catsup
2 tablespoons dry sherry
8 ounces fresh mushrooms, washed, halved and stems trimmed (try to find precut for ease)
1 onion, sliced thin
1 garlic clove, minced

Dry meat strips and toss them with salt through flour in a large plastic bag or bowl. Combine broth, catsup and sherry in **slow cooker**. Add meat and remaining ingredients through garlic and toss. Cover and cook at low temperature for 8 to 10 hours or until meat is tender.

3/4 cup fat-free sour cream
1/2 teaspoon paprika

Add sour cream and paprika, stir and heat for 15 minutes more.

Serve over rice or noodles.

22% calories from fat per serving

Yield: 6 servings
Nutrient content per serving:
Calories: 288   Fat: 7.0 g   Protein: 40.5 g   Carbohydrate: 15.8 g
Sodium: 545.4 mg   Cholesterol: 95.3 mg   Fiber: 1.4 g

Alternate Method: Spray a large skillet with nonstick cooking spray. Cook onion for about 5 minutes or until it starts to turn color. Remove onions and spray skillet again. Brown meat about 5 minutes, stirring constantly. Remove meat with a slotted spoon leaving juices in the pan. Combine broth, catsup, sherry, salt, pepper and thyme with **only** 1 1/2 tablespoons flour and add mixture to the skillet. Bring it to a simmer, add mushrooms and garlic and cook for about 5 minutes, stirring, until sauce is thickened and mushrooms are cooked. Add meat and onions and simmer, covered, for about 5 minutes more. Whisk in sour cream and paprika and heat through, but do not boil.

Greek Meatballs

A family recipe changed for today's lighter fare and the slow cooker sets you free! Bison meat is wonderful with this recipe and reduces fat content to 11 percent.

1 pound lean ground top round
2 egg whites, lightly beaten
3/4 cup onion, minced
1 cup bread crumbs, very dry
1 tablespoon lemon juice
2 tablespoons red wine
2 tablespoons fresh parsley, minced
**1 1/2 tablespoons fresh mint, minced,
   or 1 teaspoon dried mint leaves**
1/2 teaspoon cinnamon
1/2 teaspoon salt
1/8 teaspoon pepper

* Combine first 11 ingredients. (For easy mixing, place in a plastic food storage bag and squeeze.) Shape into 18 balls about 1 1/2 inches in diameter. Place in **slow cooker**.

**1 (8-ounce) can tomato sauce, low-
   sodium**
**1 (5 1/2-ounce) can vegetable juice,
   low-sodium**
1/4 cup red wine
1/4 teaspoon garlic powder
1/2 teaspoon sugar
1/4 teaspoon salt
1/8 teaspoon pepper

Combine remaining ingredients. Pour over meatballs. Cover and cook on low for 5 to 6 hours or until done.

Two teaspoons dried parsley and one teaspoon dried mint leaves may be used instead of the fresh herbs, but fresh is best, particularly in this recipe.

19% calories from fat per serving

Yield: 6 servings (3 meatballs)
Nutrient content per serving:
Calories: 216   Fat: 4.6 g   Protein: 30.3 g   Carbohydrate: 10.9 g
Sodium: 400.9 mg   Cholesterol: 68.0 mg   Fiber: 1.6 g   Alcohol: 1.4 g

Alternate Method: Combine ingredients to make meatballs as * above. Spray a shallow baking pan large enough to hold meatballs in one layer with nonstick cooking spray. Place meatballs in prepared pan and bake in a preheated 400 degree oven for about 20 to 25 minutes or until done. (Turn them halfway through cooking time.) Combine remaining ingredients in a saucepan and simmer, covered, for 20 minutes. Add cooked meatballs and cook gently for 10 minutes more.

Beef and Pepper Pockets with Cucumber Sauce

A little work, but a delightful sandwich for a summer evening.

1/4 cup lemon juice
1/4 cup red wine
1 tablespoon catsup
1 teaspoon dry mustard
1/4 teaspoon hot pepper sauce
1/2 teaspoon salt
1 garlic clove, minced
1 (1-pound) lean boneless beef
  sirloin steak, 1 1/4-inch thick
1 onion, sliced into 1/4-inch slices
1 each red and green peppers,
  cored, seeded and cut into
  1/2-inch strips

* Combine lemon juice through garlic in a heavy-duty, zip-top plastic storage bag. Add meat, onion and peppers and seal. Turn bag so vegetables and meat are coated with marinade. Refrigerate for at least 8 hours or overnight. Spray **grill** with nonstick cooking spray. Remove meat and vegetables from the marinade. Grill meat at medium high temperature for 7 to 8 minutes on each side, basting with marinade, or until done to taste. Let meat stand for 10 minutes before cutting.

2 teaspoons vegetable oil

Meanwhile, toss vegetables with the oil in a clean storage bag or bowl. Spray a grill rack with nonstick cooking spray. Cook vegetables for about 15 minutes, turning every 5 minutes, until done.

3 large pita rounds, halved

Heat pita rounds for about 1 minute in the **microwave** at high temperature until warmed slightly. ** Slice meat into thin slices, against the grain, and toss with the grilled vegetables. Spoon into pita halves, and top with cucumber sauce.

1 1/2 cups plain nonfat yogurt
1/2 cucumber, peeled, seeded and
  finely chopped (about 1/2 cup)
1/4 teaspoon salt
1 tablespoon lemon juice
1 garlic clove
1 teaspoon dried dill weed or 1
  tablespoon fresh dill, if available

Cucumber sauce: Drain yogurt (see page 235) for at least 6 hours or overnight. Combine cucumber with salt and place in a strainer for about 10 minutes. Blend drained cucumber with yogurt, lemon juice, garlic and dill in a food processor. (Or puree small batches in a blender.)

22% calories from fat per serving

Yield: 6 servings
Nutrient content per serving:
Calories: 325   Fat: 7.8 g   Protein: 30.5 g   Carbohydrate: 33.3 g
Sodium: 587.7 mg   Cholesterol: 69.8 mg   Fiber: 2.8 g

Alternate Method: Marinate meat and vegetables as * above. Spray a broiler pan with nonstick cooking spray. Broil meat, 5 to 6 inches from the heat, basting with marinade, for 7 to 8 minutes on each side. Place oil in a skillet and cook onions and peppers until done, stirring constantly. Heat pita rounds in a preheated 350 degree oven for about 5 to 10 minutes. Continue from ** above.

Eye of Round Roast in Dijon Mustard Sauce

Eye of round can be very dry due to its lack of fat. The heatproof oven bag works like magic to preserve the juices and tenderize the meat. It also shortens the cooking time.

flour
3 garlic cloves, minced
1/4 cup Dijon mustard
1/4 cup dry sherry
1/4 cup low-sodium soy sauce
1/4 cup lemon juice
1 tablespoon vegetable oil
1 teaspoon dried thyme leaves
1 teaspoon dried oregano leaves
1 (2-pound) beef eye of round roast, trimmed of all fat

Add the amount of flour to **heatproof oven bag** according to package directions. Combine garlic through oregano in a small bowl. Transfer 1/2 cup of the mixture to the oven bag along with the roast and reserve the rest. Tie. Marinate refrigerated for at least 12 hours and up to 24 hours, turning oven bag occasionally. Preheat oven to 300 degrees. Tie and vent oven bag according to package directions and place in a baking pan. Insert a meat thermometer into the roast through the oven bag. Bake for 1 hour to 1 hour 15 minutes or until the temperature is 160 degrees for medium. Remove roast from oven bag and let it rest for 15 minutes while completing the sauce. Place reserved Dijon mixture in a small saucepan and carefully pour meat juices from the oven bag into the saucepan. Bring to a boil and simmer for 2 to 3 minutes. Slice the roast against the grain and serve with the sauce.

It's so convenient to marinate and bake in the same heatproof oven bag and there is no cleanup afterwards.

31% calories from fat per serving

Yield: 8 servings

Nutrient content per serving:

Calories: 227   Fat: 7.9 g   Protein: 34.0 g   Carbohydrate: 3.1 g

Sodium: 416.0 mg   Cholesterol: 78.3 mg   Fiber: 0.2 g   Alcohol: 1.1 g

Alternate Method: Combine garlic through oregano in a large non-metal bowl. Remove all except 1/2 cup of the mixture and reserve it. Add the roast and marinate, covered and refrigerated, turning the roast occasionally, for 12 to 24 hours. Preheat oven to 325 degrees. Pour water into a broiler pan to measure 1/2 inch. Spray the broiler rack with nonstick cooking spray and place on the water-filled broiler pan. Remove roast from marinade, reserve marinade for basting, and place the roast on the broiler rack. Insert a meat thermometer. Bake for about 1 hour and 30 minutes, basting every 15 minutes with reserved marinade, or until temperature is 160 degrees for medium. Let meat rest 15 minutes. Pour marinade into a saucepan, boil for 2 to 3 minutes, add reserved mixture and boil for an additional minute. Slice the roast against the grain and serve with the sauce.

Eye of Round Fillets with Rice Noodles

Beef can be part of a low-fat meal if you chose the right cut. And the slow cooker tenderizes beautifully.

1/4 cup lemon juice
1/4 cup balsamic or red wine vinegar
1 1/2 pounds eye of round, all fat removed and cut into 6 fillets, 3/4-inch to 1-inch thick

* Combine lemon juice and vinegar in a heavy-duty zip-top plastic storage bag. Add fillets and marinate, refrigerated, overnight. Turn once, if possible. Drain and discard marinade. Place fillets in **slow cooker**.

1 cup onion, chopped
1 (14 1/2-ounce) can diced tomatoes
1/2 cup beef broth, defatted
1/2 cup red wine
1 tablespoon sugar
1/4 teaspoon ground cumin
1/2 teaspoon dry mustard
1 teaspoon dried basil leaves, crushed
1 teaspoon dried thyme leaves, crushed
1 teaspoon salt
1/4 teaspoon pepper

Combine onion through pepper and pour over fillets. Cover and cook on low for 8 hours or until tender.
** Remove fillets and keep warm.

1 (6 3/4-ounce) package rice sticks or cellophane noodles, broken into pieces

Soak rice sticks or noodles in hot water to cover for 10 minutes. Drain and add noodles to the sauce in the slow cooker. Increase heat to high. Cook for 15 minutes or until noodles are tender. Return fillets to noodle mixture.

Eliminate the noodles if desired, and serve solo with the savory tomato sauce. Replace wine with additional 1/2 cup beef broth (defatted) if desired.

14% calories from fat per serving

Yield: 6 servings
Nutrient content per serving:
Calories: 361   Fat: 5.8 g   Protein: 34.2 g   Carbohydrate: 39.9 g
Sodium: 649.1 mg   Cholesterol: 78.4 mg   Fiber: 1.4 g   Alcohol: 1.8 g

Alternate Method: Combine ingredients and marinate fillets as * above. Drain and discard marinade. Combine onion through pepper in a Dutch oven. Add fillets. Bring to a boil, reduce to a simmer, and cook covered for 1 to 1 1/2 hours or until tender. Continue as ** above using the Dutch oven instead of the slow cooker and reduce final cooking time to 5 minutes.

Leg of Lamb With Red Pepper Sauce

Moist, juicy, no watching and basting, this is a wonderful way to cook this delightful cut of meat for a crowd and still be part of the party.

flour
1 (4 1/2-pound) leg of lamb, boned, rolled and tied
2 garlic cloves, each cut into 8 slivers
2 tablespoons Dijon mustard
1 tablespoon low-sodium soy sauce
1 teaspoon dried thyme leaves

Preheat oven to 300 degrees. Add the amount of flour to **heatproof oven bag** according to package directions. * Dry lamb with paper towels. Make 16 small slits in the lamb with a sharp knife. Insert a sliver of garlic into each slit. Combine mustard, thyme and soy sauce and rub over meat. Place lamb in the oven bag. Tie and vent according to package directions and place in a baking pan. Insert meat thermometer into lamb through the oven bag. Bake for about 1 hour and 45 minutes to 2 hours or until the temperature is 170 degrees for medium. Let rest for 10 minutes before slicing. Remove the tie string. Discard juices in oven bag and serve with pepper sauce.

3 (7-ounce jars) roasted red peppers, drained
3 tablespoons Dijon mustard
3 tablespoons plain nonfat yogurt
3 tablespoons lemon juice
3 tablespoons fresh parsley, minced
3 garlic cloves
3 teaspoons sugar
3/4 teaspoon salt
1/8 teaspoon pepper

Pepper Sauce: Combine red peppers through pepper in a food processor and blend until smooth. (Or puree small batches in a blender.) Serve sauce at room temperature.

Since servings are slightly more than the 30% fat guideline, serve this with a low-fat vegetable dish to reduce fat percentage for the meal. This is one of the leanest cuts of lamb, so enjoy! Freeze leftovers in a new heatproof oven bag. Refer to "Storage Uses of the Heatproof Oven Bag", page 231.

33% calories from fat per serving

Yield: 18 servings

Nutrient content per serving:

Calories: 218   Fat: 7.9 g   Protein: 32.4 g   Carbohydrate: 4.2 g

Sodium: 297.7 mg   Cholesterol: 98.9 mg   Fiber: 0.1 g

Alternate Method: Preheat oven to 325 degrees. Prepare and roast lamb as * above, but place it directly in a roasting pan and baste frequently until temperature is 170 degrees for medium.

Ramen Noodles With Black Beans and Beef

This recipe is so easy; even a child could prepare it.

3/4 pound lean ground top round
1 (2 1/2-ounce) package low-fat
   ramen noodles
1 (14 1/2-ounce) can stewed
   tomatoes, with liquid
1 (15-ounce) can black beans,
   drained and rinsed
3/4 cup low-sodium vegetable juice
1 teaspoon Worcestershire sauce
1 teaspoon dried oregano leaves
1/4 teaspoon garlic powder
3/4 teaspoon salt
1/8 teaspoon pepper

Spread meat evenly on the bottom of a 3-quart **microwave**-safe casserole. Cover and cook at high temperature in the microwave for 4 minutes, stirring and crumbling after each 2 minutes, until browned. Drain the liquid which has been produced. Crush the noodles and discard the sauce packet. (For ease, crush the noodles in the packet **before** opening.) Combine noodles with meat along with the remaining ingredients. Cover and cook at high temperature for 5 to 7 minutes or until mixture comes to a simmer. Stir. Cook at medium low heat (30% power) for an additional 5 minutes or until noodles are tender. Let rest 5 minutes. Stir before serving. (Rotate casserole 1/2 turn halfway through each cooking period if microwave does not have a carousel.)

14% calories from fat per serving

Yield: 6 servings

Nutrient content per serving:
Calories: 209   Fat: 3.3 g   Protein: 18.4 g   Carbohydrate: 26.3 g
Sodium: 802 mg   Cholesterol: 28.0 mg   Fiber: 5.1 g

Alternate Method: Coat a large, nonstick casserole with nonstick cooking spray. Cook meat, stirring to crumble, until browned. Drain liquid and add remaining ingredients. Bring to a boil, reduce heat and simmer, covered, for 10 to 15 minutes or until noodles are tender.

Main Dishes
Pork

Notes

_____ _____

_____ _____

_____ _____

_____ _____

_____ _____

_____ _____

_____ _____

_____ _____

_____ _____

_____ _____

_____ _____

_____ _____

_____ _____

Pork Stew with Lentils, Raisins and Dried Apples

Make this stew a day ahead for the wonderful flavors to blend. Serve over noodles.

2 pounds pork top loin, cut into 1 1/2-inch cubes
1 (28-ounce) can diced tomatoes
1 onion, chopped
1/2 cup golden raisins
1/2 cup dried apples
1 teaspoon salt
1/4 teaspoon pepper
1/4 teaspoon nutmeg
1/2 teaspoon dried thyme leaves
1 teaspoon dried mint leaves

Combine pork through mint in the **slow cooker**. Cover and cook at low temperature for 8 to 10 hours or until meat is tender.

1 cup brown lentils
3 cups water

Meanwhile, cook lentils and water in **rice cooker** for 30 minutes or until just tender. Drain. Combine lentils with stew before serving.

20% calories from fat per serving

Yield: 8 (1 1/2-cup) servings

Nutrient content per serving:
Calories: 378   Fat: 8.6 g   Protein: 42.7 g   Carbohydrate: 32.5 g
Sodium: 519.6 mg   Cholesterol: 88.1 mg   Fiber: 9.7 g

Alternate Method: Spray a Dutch oven with nonstick cooking spray and brown pork, stirring constantly. Add tomatoes through mint and combine. Bring to a boil, reduce to a simmer, cover and bake in a preheated 350 degree oven for 1 1/4 to 1 1/2 hours, stirring occasionally, until pork is tender. Meanwhile, bring lentils and water to a boil in a saucepan. Reduce heat, cover and simmer for 20 to 30 minutes or until just tender. Drain. Combine lentils with stew before serving.

Old-Fashioned Roast Pork

The heatproof oven bag produces an incredibly tender pork roast. The juices which accumulate in the oven bag make a lovely sauce. (It's so easy to skim the fat; pan-roasted pork roast not utilizing the oven bag will yield "drippings" which cannot easily be defatted.)

1 teaspoon salt
1/8 teaspoon pepper
1/2 teaspoon dried thyme leaves
1/4 teaspoon garlic powder
1 (3-pound) boneless double pork
   loin roast (all fat removed), tied
flour
2 small onions, quartered

* Combine salt through garlic powder. Rub on roast. Cover tightly and refrigerate several hours to marinate, if possible. Preheat oven to 300 degrees. Add the amount of flour to **heatproof oven bag** according to package directions. Place roast and onions in the oven bag. Tie and vent according to package directions and place in a baking pan. Insert a meat thermometer into the roast through the oven bag. Bake for 30 to 40 minutes a pound or until the temperature is 180 degrees for well done. Remove roast from the oven bag and let it rest for 15 minutes while completing the sauce. Pour juices in the bag carefully into a gravy skimmer and remove all rendered fat.

1 tablespoon cornstarch
1 tablespoon water

To further thicken juices, transfer to a **microwave**-safe bowl, then follow method on page 236. (These measurements are for 1 cup juices; increase proportionately, if necessary.) Slice meat against the grain and serve with the juices and onions.

Serve this with a low-fat vegetable dish to reduce fat percentage for the meal. For later eating, freeze the roast in its oven bag. Refer to "Storage Uses of the Heatproof Oven Bag" on page 231 for details.

33% calories from fat per serving

Yield: 12 servings
Nutrient content per serving:

Calories: 221   Fat: 8.2 g   Protein: 34.5 g   Carbohydrate: 2.4 g

Sodium: 245.2 mg   Cholesterol: 88.1 mg   Fiber: 0.4 g

Alternate Method: Rub roast with herbs and marinate as * above. Spray a large baking pan with nonstick cooking spray. Place the roast in the pan and surround with onions. Insert a meat thermometer in the roast. Bake for 35 to 40 minutes per pound or until temperature is 180 degrees for well done. Baste frequently with pan juices.

Pork Kebabs with Pineapple in Minted Yogurt Marinade

A marinade with a Mediterranean flavor enhances this wonderful cut of pork.

1 1/3 cups plain, nonfat yogurt
1/2 cup fresh mint, minced
1 tablespoon lemon juice
3 garlic cloves, minced
1/2 teaspoon ground ginger
1/4 teaspoon salt
dash red pepper sauce

1 1/2 pounds pork top loin, cut
   into 1-inch cubes
1 pound pineapple, cut into 1-inch
   cubes (buy packaged precut, if
   possible)
1/2 red onion, quartered and
   separated into layers
6 wooden skewers, soaked in
   water for at least 30 minutes
3 lemons, quartered

* Combine yogurt through pepper sauce in a large glass bowl. Remove and reserve 2/3 cup of the mixture.

Combine pork with yogurt mixture in the bowl. Cover and marinate refrigerated for at least 6 hours or overnight. Remove pork from marinade, leaving a thin coat on the meat. Brush pineapple and onion lightly with some of the marinade. Alternate pork, pineapple, and onion on skewers. Spray **grill** with nonstick cooking spray. Grill over medium heat for 5 to 10 minutes on each side or until center is not pink but still juicy. ** Brush with marinade when turning. Serve with reserved yogurt mixture and lemon wedges.

Fresh mint is really best in this recipe, but substitute 3 tablespoons dried mint leaves, if necessary.

24% calories from fat per serving

Yield: 6 servings
Nutrient content per serving:
Calories: 326   Fat: 8.8 g   Protein: 38.5 g   Carbohydrate: 23.2 g
Sodium: 194.7 mg   Cholesterol: 90.7 mg   Fiber: 1.4 g

Alternate Method: Marinate pork and assemble as * above. Spray a broiler pan with nonstick cooking spray. Broil under medium broiler, 5 to 6 inches from the heat for 5 to 10 minutes on each side. Continue as ** above. Watch carefully to avoid overcooking.

Ham Cutlets with Plum Sauce

Relatively high in sodium, smoked ham can be a part of your low-fat fare if eaten occasionally.

1 (1-pound) can purple plums in heavy syrup
1 tablespoon lemon juice
1 tablespoon maple syrup
1 teaspoon Dijon mustard
2 (1-pound) cooked, boneless ham steaks, 1/2-inch thick, all fat trimmed, each cut into 4 cutlets

Spray **grill** with nonstick cooking spray. * Drain plums and reserve syrup. Pit plums and combine with lemon juice, maple syrup and mustard along with 3 tablespoons reserved plum syrup in a food processor or blender. Puree. Brush ham cutlets with plum mixture and grill over medium heat for 5 minutes on each side, basting before and after turning. Add 2 more tablespoons reserved plum syrup to plum mixture, place in a small **microwave**-safe bowl, cover and microwave at high temperature for 2 minutes or until mixture simmers for at least one minute. Serve ham with the plum sauce.

26% calories from fat per serving

Yield: 8 servings

Nutrient content per serving:

Calories: 220   Fat: 6.3 g   Protein: 28.7 g   Carbohydrate: 12.0 g
Sodium: 1520 mg   Cholesterol: 62.4 mg   Fiber: 0.6 g

Alternate Method: Puree plums through mustard as * above. Spray a broiler pan with nonstick cooking spray. Brush ham cutlets with plum mixture and broil under medium broiler 5 to 6 inches from the heat for about 5 minutes on each side. Baste before and after turning. Add 2 more tablespoons reserved plum syrup to plum mixture and simmer in a small saucepan for at least one minute, stirring.

Pork Tenderloin in Beer Sauce

Substitute defatted chicken broth for beer, if desired.

1 1/2 pounds pork tenderloin, cut into 1-inch cubes
1/2 cup chicken broth, defatted
3/4 cup beer
1 tablespoon Worcestershire sauce
1 tablespoon vinegar
1 tablespoon sugar
1 tablespoon vegetable oil
1 onion, sliced thin
2 garlic cloves, minced
1 teaspoon dried thyme leaves
1 teaspoon paprika
1 teaspoon salt
1/8 teaspoon pepper

Combine all ingredients in a **slow cooker**. Cover and cook at low temperature for 7 hours or until pork is cooked. (It should not be pink.) Stir before serving.

If desired, thicken juices according to method on page 236. Very good over rice.

29% calories from fat per serving

Yield: 6 servings

Nutrient content per serving:

Calories: 202   Fat: 6.5 g   Protein: 26.0 g   Carbohydrate: 7.9 g
Sodium: 474.7 mg   Cholesterol: 59.1 mg   Fiber: 1.0 g   Alcohol: 1.1 g

Alternate Method: Spray a large Dutch oven with nonstick cooking spray and brown the pork, stirring. Add remaining ingredients. Bring to a simmer, cover and bake in a preheated 300 degree oven for 1 hour to 1 hour 15 minutes or until pork is cooked. (It should not be pink.)

Braised Pork Loin Roast with Tomatoes and Mushrooms

This roast is good enough to serve for a special meal, and you can ignore it all day long while it's cooking.

1 (3-pound) boneless double pork loin roast, tied, all fat removed
1 teaspoon dried thyme leaves
1 teaspoon dried basil leaves
1/4 teaspoon garlic powder
1/2 teaspoon salt
1/4 teaspoon pepper

* Dry pork in paper towels and rub with combined seasonings. Place in a **slow cooker**.

1 (14 1/2-ounce) can Italian plum tomatoes
8 ounces mushrooms, washed, trimmed and halved if small or quartered if large
1/2 cup sliced celery
1/2 cup dry red wine
1 teaspoon salt
1/8 teaspoon pepper

Combine remaining ingredients and pour over pork. Cover and cook at low setting for 8 to 10 hours or until an instant-read thermometer registers 170 degrees for medium. ** Remove the roast to a platter, remove the tie string and surround it with vegetables. Transfer remaining juices in the slow cooker to a gravy skimmer, remove all fat, pour a little of the juices over the pork and pass the rest.

This is slightly over the 30% fat guideline, but so close and so good that it's included. Serve with a very low-fat vegetable dish to reduce fat percentage for the meal.

32% calories from fat per serving

Yield: 12 servings
Nutrient content per serving:
Calories: 231   Fat: 8.3 g   Protein: 34.9 g   Carbohydrate: 2.4 g
Sodium: 413.3 mg   Cholesterol: 88.1 mg   Fiber: 0.6 g   Alcohol: 1.0 g

Alternate Method: Prepare the roast as * above. Spray a large Dutch oven with nonstick cooking spray and brown the roast on all sides. Combine tomatoes through pepper and pour over the roast. Bring liquid to a simmer, cover and bake in a preheated 325 degree oven for about 2 hours or until an instant-read thermometer registers 170 degrees. Baste with pan juices every 30 minutes. Continue as ** above.

Pork Tenderloin in Soy Marinade

The heatproof oven bag does the basting to keep this low-fat cut of pork moist.

2 (3/4-pound) pork tenderloins
flour
1/3 cup low-sodium soy sauce
1/4 cup sugar
1 tablespoon lemon juice
1 tablespoon vegetable oil
1/8 teaspoon pepper
1 large onion, cut into 6 wedges

Trim fat from pork. Dry the meat with paper towels. Add the amount of flour to a **heatproof oven bag** according to package directions. Combine soy sauce through pepper in the oven bag, add pork, tie and marinate for at least 6 hours, refrigerated. Preheat oven to 300 degrees. Add onions to the oven bag. Tie and vent according to package directions and place the oven bag in a baking pan. Insert a meat thermometer in the meat through the oven bag. Bake for 40 to 45 minutes or until the temperature is 170 degrees. Remove pork and onions from the oven bag and let the pork rest while completing the sauce. Pour juices carefully into a gravy skimmer and remove all rendered fat.

1 tablespoon cornstarch
1 tablespoon red wine or water

* To further thicken juices, transfer to a **microwave**-safe bowl, then follow method on page 236. (These measurements are for 1 cup juices; increase proportionately, if necessary.) Season sauce to taste. Slice meat diagonally into 1/2-inch slices and serve with the sauce and onions.

Serve juices without thickening, if desired, but simmer for at least 2 minutes.

26% calories from fat per serving

Yield: 6 servings

Nutrient content per serving:

Calories: 229   Fat: 6.5 g   Protein: 26.4 g   Carbohydrate: 16.1 g

Sodium: 591.9 mg   Cholesterol: 59.1 mg   Fiber: 0.8 g

Alternate Method: Trim fat from pork and dry. Combine soy sauce through pepper in a non-metal bowl, add pork and marinate, covered and refrigerated, for at least 6 hours. Place pork and onions in a roasting pan, reserve marinade, insert a meat thermometer in pork and bake at 325 degrees for 40 to 45 minutes until temperature is 170 degrees. Baste frequently with the reserved marinade. Skim fat from the juices and continue as * above.

Herbed Pork Chops in Tomato Sauce

So tender, so easy, so good.

1 1/2 pounds lean boneless top loin pork chops, about 6 (4-ounce) chops
1 teaspoon Seed Rub (page 208)
1/2 cup chicken broth, defatted

1/2 cup tomato sauce
1/2 cup chicken broth, defatted
1 teaspoon Seed Rub (page 208)
1 tablespoon cornstarch
1 tablespoon red wine

* Rub chops on both sides with 1 teaspoon Seed Rub and place them in a **slow cooker**. Pour the broth over chops and cover. Cook at low temperature for 7 to 8 hours or until tender. Discard liquid.

Combine tomato sauce, broth and Seed Rub in a small **microwave**-safe bowl. Heat in the microwave for 1 minute on high. Combine cornstarch and red wine and add to the heated sauce. Heat in microwave on high for 1 minute. Stir. Heat another minute or until slightly thickened. Pour over chops in the slow cooker and cook at high temperature for 20 to 30 minutes, covered, or until some of the sauce has been absorbed by the chops.

Serve chops with a low-fat side dish to reduce fat percentage for the meal.

33% calories from fat per serving

Yield: 6 servings
Nutrient content per serving:
Calories: 228   Fat: 8.3 g   Protein: 35.6 g   Carbohydrate: 2.8 g
Sodium: 192.5 mg   Cholesterol: 88.5 mg   Fiber: 0.3 g

Alternate Method: Preheat oven to 350 degrees. Rub chops as * above and place in a 2-quart casserole. Pour 1/2 cup broth over chops and bake, covered, for 1 hour or until tender. Discard liquid. Heat remaining 1/2 cup broth with 1 teaspoon Seed Rub and tomato sauce in a small saucepan until warm. Combine cornstarch and wine and add to saucepan. Bring to a simmer, stirring, and heat until slightly thickened. Pour over chops, cover and bake for 20 to 30 minutes more or until the chops have absorbed some of the sauce.

Pork Tenderloins with Chutney Sauce

These grilled tenderloins have a crusty coating and a very moist center.

2 (3/4-pound) pork tenderloins
1 tablespoon vegetable oil
1/4 cup lemon juice
2 tablespoons catsup
2 tablespoons honey
1 tablespoon dry sherry
1 1/2 teaspoons curry powder
1 teaspoon ground cumin
2 garlic cloves, minced

* Trim all fat from the tenderloins. Combine oil through garlic in a heavy-duty zip-top plastic storage bag. Add pork. Seal. Toss to cover pork with marinade. Refrigerate about 8 hours, turning once or twice during this period. (Marinate in a glass bowl, if desired.) Remove pork and reserve marinade. Spray **grill** with nonstick cooking spray. Grill at medium-low temperature on a preheated grill for about 25 minutes or until an instant-read thermometer registers 160 degrees. Turn and baste with reserved marinade at least once while grilling. ** Transfer the pork to a cutting board and allow it to rest for 10 minutes. Discard the marinade. Cut pork diagonally into 1/2-inch slices.

1/2 cup fat-free sour cream
1/2 cup mango chutney
1/2 teaspoon curry powder
1 tablespoon fresh chives, minced

Combine the remaining ingredients and serve the sauce with the pork.

For later eating, freeze in a heatproof oven bag. Refer to "Storage Uses of the Heatproof Oven Bag" on page 231 for details.

22% calories from fat per serving

Yield: 6 servings

Nutrient content per serving:

Calories: 271   Fat: 6.6 g   Protein: 26.5 g   Carbohydrate: 26.4 g
Sodium: 248.5 mg   Cholesterol: 59.1 mg   Fiber: 1.1 g

Alternate Method: Marinate the pork as * above. Remove pork from marinade and place in a baking pan. Before cooking, bring pork to room temperature. Insert a meat thermometer. Roast in a preheated 300 degree oven for about 1 hour, basting every 15 minutes with reserved marinade, or until temperature is 160 degrees. Continue as ** above.

Grilled Pork Chops with Spice Rub

The boneless sirloin chop is second only to the tenderloin for low fat content. Ask the butcher for this cut and enjoy pork more frequently.

6 (4-ounce) boneless sirloin chops,
   1/2-inch thick
1 tablespoon dried oregano leaves
1 teaspoon curry powder
1 teaspoon ground cumin
1/2 teaspoon cinnamon
1 teaspoon paprika
1 teaspoon salt
1/4 teaspoon pepper

Lemon wedges

* Trim all fat from chops. Pat dry with paper towels. Combine herbs and spices and rub on both sides of the chops. Refrigerate, covered, for 8 to 24 hours. Spray **grill** with nonstick cooking spray. Grill over medium-high heat for about 5 minutes on each side or until the pork is just cooked through.

Pass the lemon wedges for a tangy flavor.

Even though the fat percentage is slightly over 30%, this relatively low-fat pork recipe is included. Serve with a low-fat vegetable dish to reduce fat percentage for the meal.

32% calories from fat per serving

Yield: 6 servings
Nutrient content per serving:
Calories: 218   Fat: 7.8 g   Protein: 35.6 g   Carbohydrate: 1.3 g
Sodium: 453.0 mg   Cholesterol: 104.1 mg   Fiber: 0.6 g

Alternate Method: Prepare chops and marinate as * above. Spray a broiler pan with nonstick cooking spray. Broil chops 5 to 6 inches from heat in a preheated broiler for about 5 minutes on each side. Serve with lemon wedges.

Main Dishes
Fish and Shellfish

Notes

_____   _____
_____   _____
_____   _____
_____   _____
_____   _____
_____   _____
_____   _____
_____   _____
_____   _____
_____   _____
_____   _____
_____   _____
_____   _____
_____   _____
_____   _____
_____   _____

Spicy Tuna Steaks

The thickness of this steak will ensure its juiciness. Don't cook too fast, and don't overcook!

3 tablespoons lemon juice
2 tablespoons olive oil
1 tablespoon dry mustard
1 tablespoon chili powder
1/2 teaspoon salt
1 teaspoon pepper
6 (4-ounce) yellowfin tuna steaks,
   1 1/2-inches thick

* Combine lemon juice through pepper in a zip-top plastic storage bag. Add tuna steaks, seal, and marinate, covered and refrigerated, for at least 30 minutes and up to 2 hours. Spray **grill** with nonstick cooking spray. ** Remove fish from marinade and grill at medium heat for a total of 15 minutes, turning once, or until fish flakes easily with a fork. Baste with reserved marinade before turning.

28% calories from fat per serving

Yield: 6 servings
Nutrient content per serving:
Calories: 202   Fat: 6.4 g   Protein: 34.4 g   Carbohydrate: 1.7 g
Sodium: 260.5 mg   Cholesterol: 65.7 mg   Fiber: 0.6 g

Alternate Method: Marinate steaks as * above. Spray broiler pan with nonstick cooking spray. Broil steaks under medium broiler, 6 to 7 inches from the heat, basting and turning as ** above. Watch carefully to avoid overcooking.

Scallops With Curried Clam Sauce

Don't overlook the "low in fat" sea scallop for an easy, elegant evening meal.

1 cup bottled clam juice
1/4 cup water
2 tablespoons green onions, minced
1 pound fresh sea scallops (about 1-inch diameter), patted dry

Spray **rice cooker** container and steamer plate with nonstick cooking spray. * Place clam juice, water and onions into container and insert steamer plate. Liquid should not cover plate. (If necessary, place a small can or rack under steamer plate to raise it to desired level.) Place scallops directly on the steamer plate. Cover and turn on machine. Start timing when liquid begins to steam (about 5 minutes). Steam for 5 minutes longer or until scallops are just firm to the touch. Remove them and keep warm while completing sauce.

1 tablespoon cornstarch
1 tablespoon white wine
1 teaspoon curry powder
1/4 teaspoon salt
1/8 teaspoon pepper
1/4 cup mango chutney

Combine cornstarch and wine. Carefully remove rice cooker container with broth from rice cooker. Whisk in cornstarch mixture until blended. Return container to cooker, add curry powder through pepper, and simmer, stirring, for 2 minutes or until thickened. Add chutney. Stir. Remove from heat and toss with scallops.

8% calories from fat per serving

Yield: 4 servings

Nutrient content per serving:
Calories: 153   Fat: 1.4 g   Protein: 21.2 g   Carbohydrate: 13.9 g
Sodium: 530.7 mg   Cholesterol: 48.2 mg   Fiber: 0.7 g

Alternate Method: Use a vegetable steamer basket which fits in a large pot and continue as * above. Cook on the stove and use the pot instead of the rice cooker container in all steps.

Steamed Gingered Salmon with Orange Sauce

The rice cooker is wonderful when used as a steamer. A note about salmon: it's not a low-fat fish. Pink salmon is lower in fat, but Atlantic salmon is easier to find, so the nutrition values are for the Atlantic salmon.

4 (4-ounce) Atlantic, farm-raised, salmon steaks, 1-inch thick
1/4 teaspoon ginger
1/4 teaspoon salt
1/8 teaspoon pepper
3/4 cup water
3/4 cup white wine or chicken broth, defatted

Spray **rice cooker** container and steamer plate with nonstick cooking spray. * Pour water and wine into container and insert steamer plate. Water level should not come above plate. (If necessary, place a small can or rack under steamer plate to raise it to desired level.) Sprinkle steaks with ginger, salt and pepper. Place steaks directly on steamer plate. Cover rice cooker and turn on machine. Start timing when liquid begins to steam (about 5 minutes). Steam for 10 minutes longer or until fish just flakes easily with a fork.

3 tablespoons orange marmalade
2 tablespoons Dijon mustard
1/2 teaspoon ginger
1/4 cup chicken broth, defatted

Combine marmalade through chicken broth in a **microwave**-safe bowl. Cover and cook in the microwave for about 30 seconds on high until mixture comes to a simmer. Serve over salmon.

Wine calories are not included since the wine is used only for steaming.

33% calories from fat per serving

Yield: 4 servings
Nutrient content per serving:
Calories: 212   Fat: 7.8 g   Protein: 23.5 g   Carbohydrate: 12.0 g
Sodium: 244.7 mg   Cholesterol: 62.4 mg   Fiber: 1.0 g

Alternate Method: Use a vegetable steamer basket which fits in a large pot and continue as * above. Cook on the stove and use the pot instead of the rice cooker container in all steps. Combine marmalade through broth in a small saucepan and simmer for 2 minutes, stirring. Serve over salmon.

Shrimp and Orzo with Tarragon

This creamy orzo dish will remind you of risotto; but you won't miss the stirring and cleanup using the heatproof oven bag.

flour
1 cup orzo (rice-shaped) pasta
3 1/2 cups chicken broth, defatted
1/2 cup white wine
1 bay leaf
3/4 teaspoon dried tarragon leaves
1/8 teaspoon pepper

Preheat oven to 400 degrees. Add the amount of flour to a **heatproof oven bag** according to package directions. Combine orzo pasta through pepper in the oven bag. Place in a baking pan and tie and vent according to package directions. * Bake for about 15 minutes or until liquid just begins to simmer. Reduce heat to 350 degrees and bake another 45 minutes or until liquid is nearly absorbed. (Pasta mixture should not be totally dry.) Carefully remove bay leaf.

12 ounces small or medium-size shrimp, cooked, peeled and deveined (use frozen precooked shrimp for convenience)
1 teaspoon Old Bay Seasoning

In the meantime, sprinkle shrimp with Old Bay Seasoning. Add shrimp to the pasta. Retie oven bag and let pasta sit for 10 minutes to warm shrimp.

4 teaspoons Parmesan cheese

Sprinkle each serving with 1 teaspoon Parmesan cheese.

Eliminate wine and increase chicken broth to 4 cups, if desired.

4% calories from fat per serving

Yield: 4 servings
Nutrient content per serving:
Calories: 273   Fat: 1.3 g   Protein: 28.4 g   Carbohydrate: 32.2 g
Sodium: 805.6 mg   Cholesterol: 138.5 mg   Fiber: 1.6 g   Alcohol: 2.7 g

Alternate Method: Preheat oven to 400 degrees. Combine broth through pepper in a saucepan and bring it to a boil. Add orzo pasta and stir. Transfer mixture to a baking pan which has been sprayed with nonstick cooking spray. Cover. Bake as * above, stirring occasionally until pasta is done and liquid is nearly absorbed. Sprinkle shrimp with seasoning and add it to the pan, cover, and let sit for 10 minutes to warm shrimp. Remove bay leaf. Serve topped with cheese.

Grouper with Black Beans

Use any mild white fish and this method to produce a succulent fish dinner. Fish is always moist when cooked in a heatproof oven bag!

flour
1 (1-pound) can black beans,
   drained and rinsed
1/4 cup chicken broth, defatted
2 tablespoons lemon juice
1 teaspoon ground cumin
1/4 teaspoon salt
dash pepper

4 (4-ounce) grouper fillets, about
   1-inch thick
1 small onion, thinly sliced
4 parsley springs
1 tablespoon vegetable oil

Preheat oven to 400 degrees. Add the amount of flour to a **heatproof oven bag** according to package directions. Allow flour to settle in one corner and place in a baking pan. Combine beans through pepper in a bowl and transfer to the oven bag, spreading beans evenly across the bottom.

Place grouper on beans. Separate onion into rings and spread over grouper. Top with parsley and drizzle with oil. Tie and vent according to package directions. Bake for 20 to 30 minutes or until grouper springs back when touched lightly through the oven bag. Slit bag. * Remove grouper fillets carefully to serving plates. Top with beans and onions. (Cooking time will depend on thickness of fish.)

20% calories from fat per serving

Yield: 4 servings
Nutrient content per serving:
Calories: 255   Fat: 5.6 g   Protein: 29.3 g   Carbohydrate: 21.8 g
Sodium: 545.9 mg   Cholesterol: 41.6 mg   Fiber: 7.2 g

Alternate Method: Spray a heatproof casserole just large enough to hold the grouper in one layer with non-stick cooking spray. Combine beans through pepper and spread in casserole. Top with grouper. Separate onion into rings and spread over grouper. Top with parsley and drizzle with oil. Cover. Bake in a preheated 425 degree oven for 20 to 25 minutes or until grouper flakes easily with a fork. Continue from * above.

Halibut Steak with Tarragon

A quick, tasty meal. Swordfish steaks can be used instead of halibut. Do not overcook.

4 (4-ounce) halibut steaks, 1-inch thick
2 tablespoons lemon juice
1 1/2 teaspoons dried tarragon leaves
1/2 teaspoon garlic powder

* Rub both sides of halibut with tarragon and garlic powder and drizzle with lemon juice. Place in a heavy-duty zip-top plastic storage bag and marinate at cool room temperature for 30 minutes or refrigerate for about 2 hours. Spray a **grill** rack with nonstick cooking spray. Place halibut on rack and grill (indirect heat if possible) at medium high heat for 5 to 7 minutes on each side, depending on thickness. ** Baste with marinade mixture. Spray halibut lightly with nonstick cooking spray before turning. Remove carefully.

2 tablespoons lemon juice

Drizzle with additional lemon juice before serving.

Serve with "Yogurt Paprika Sauce" (page 195), if desired.

19% calories from fat per serving

Yield: 4 servings
Nutrient content per serving:
Calories: 123   Fat: 2.6 g   Protein: 23.8 g   Carbohydrate: 1.1 g
Sodium: 61.8 mg   Cholesterol: 36.3 mg   Fiber: 0.1 g

Alternate Method: Marinate halibut as * above. Spray a broiler rack with nonstick cooking spray. Broil at medium high heat 5 to 6 inches from the heat for 5 to 7 minutes on each side, depending on thickness. Continue as ** above.

Grilled Flounder With Pineapple Slices

The "grill basket" is invaluable when grilling delicate varieties of fish.

2 tablespoons vegetable oil
1/4 cup lemon juice
1 teaspoon dried tarragon leaves
1/2 teaspoon salt
1/8 teaspoon pepper
6 (4-ounce) flounder fillets
1 (1-pound) can pineapple slices,
   juice-packed, drained

Grill basket

Combine oil through pepper in a heavy-duty zip-top plastic storage bag. Dry fillets and add to the bag along with the pineapple slices. Seal. Turn bag so juices cover all sides of fish and pineapple. Marinate 30 minutes to 1 hour, refrigerated.

Preheat the **grill** to medium high. Spray the grill basket well with nonstick cooking spray. Place the fillets in the basket, baste with marinade, fasten basket and place the basket on the grill. Baste pineapple slices with marinade and place them directly on the grill. Cook both fillets and pineapple for about 5 minutes on each side, basting after turning and also again just before removing from the heat.
* Top each fillet with a slice of pineapple and serve immediately.

26% calories from fat per serving

Yield: 6 servings
Nutrient content per serving:
Calories: 221 Fat: 6.4 g Protein: 27.8 g Carbohydrate: 13.0 g
Sodium: 313.8 mg Cholesterol: 77.1 mg Fiber: 0.6 g

Alternate Method: Preheat oven to 350 degrees. Spray a baking dish, large enough to hold the fillets in one layer, with nonstick cooking spray. Place fillets in baking dish. Combine oil through pepper and pour over fillets, reserving about 1 tablespoon to baste pineapple. Cover with foil. Bake for 25 to 30 minutes or until fish flakes easily with a fork. Meanwhile, place pineapple in a broiler pan which has been sprayed with nonstick cooking spray. Brush with reserved marinade and broil 5 to 6 inches from the heat for about 5 minutes or until lightly browned. Continue from * above.

Shrimp with Tomatoes and Feta

Use frozen, cooked shrimp in this almost effortless delicious dish. Cook and serve from the same casserole.

1/2 cup chopped onions
2 garlic cloves, minced
1/4 cup chicken broth, defatted
1 (14 1/2-ounce) can diced tomatoes
1/2 cup tomato sauce
1 teaspoon dried basil leaves
1 teaspoon dry mustard
1 teaspoon sugar
1 tablespoon fresh parsley, minced
2 tablespoons white wine
1/2 teaspoon salt
1/8 teaspoon pepper

Place onions, garlic and broth in a **microwave**-safe 3-quart casserole. Cover and cook at high temperature in the microwave for 3 minutes or until onion is softened. Add tomatoes through pepper and cook, covered, for 10 minutes. (Rotate 1/2 turn halfway through cooking time if microwave does not have a carousel.)

1 pound frozen cooked medium-sized shrimp, shelled, deveined and defrosted according to package instructions

Add shrimp, cover, and cook for 5 minutes more. (Rotate again, if necessary, if microwave does not have a carousel.)

4 ounces crumbled feta cheese

* Top casserole with feta and broil 7 inches from heat for 5 minutes or just until cheese is melted.

1 1/2 cups long-grain white rice

Meanwhile, cook rice in the **rice cooker** (page 234) or stovetop per package directions and serve shrimp over rice.

This dish is relatively high in both sodium and cholesterol, but the American Heart Association approves a 3-ounce serving of shrimp or lobster each week.

14% calories from fat per serving

Yield: 6 servings

Nutrient content per serving:

Calories: 298   Fat: 4.5 g   Protein: 22.2 g   Carbohydrate: 42.1 g
Sodium: 1067 mg   Cholesterol: 138.7 mg   Fiber: 1.4 g

Alternate Method: Spray a large saucepan with nonstick cooking spray. Cook onions and garlic over low heat, stirring constantly, until softened. Add broth through pepper, bring to a boil, reduce to a simmer, and cook, covered, for 15 minutes. Add shrimp and cook 5 minutes more. Spray a 10x14-inch casserole with nonstick cooking spray. Turn shrimp mixture into prepared casserole. Continue as * above.

Tilapia Fillets on Asparagus

Fish stays so moist when cooked in the microwave and no extra fat is required. A one-dish effort - cook the asparagus and fish in the same dish!

1 pound asparagus spears

Wash asparagus and snap off the tough ends. Arrange lengthwise in a rectangular **microwave**-safe dish (about 12x8x2 inches). Add 2 table-spoons water. (Asparagus tips should point to the center of the dish.) Cover tightly. Microwave on high for 3 min-utes or until asparagus is crisp-tender.

2 tablespoons lemon juice
1 tablespoon dry vermouth or apple
** juice**
1/2 teaspoon paprika
1/2 teaspoon salt
6 (4-ounce) tilapia fillets,
** patted dry**
2 tablespoons minced fresh parsley

* Combine lemon juice through salt and brush mixture on both sides of fillets. Place fillets on asparagus. Sprinkle with parsley. Cover tightly. Microwave on high for 6 to 7 minutes or until fillets flake easily with a fork. (Rotate dish 1/2 turn halfway through cooking time if microwave does not have a carousel.)

Serve with Roasted Red Pepper Sauce (page 196), if desired.

Tilapia is also called "bream" in some areas of the country. If this mild fish is not avail-able, substitute any white fish.

17% calories from fat per serving

Yield: 6 servings
Nutrient content per serving:
Calories: 124   Fat: 2.4 g   Protein: 23.7 g   Carbohydrate: 1.8 g
Sodium: 236.7 mg   Cholesterol: 0.0 mg   Fiber: 1.0 g

Alternate Method: Cook trimmed asparagus in boiling water 3 to 4 minutes or until just crisp-tender. Refresh under cold water. Drain. Place in a rectangular baking dish. Prepare fillets and arrange on asparagus as * above. Cover. Bake in a preheated 350 degree oven for 25 to 30 minutes or until fillets flake easily with a fork.

Side Dishes

Vegetables and Fruits

Side Dishes

Vegetables and Fruits

Cabbage and Beet Oriental

So simple using packaged cole slaw (found in the produce section of the market), this is a quick route to an unusual side dish. It's high in vitamin A with 521 RE units per serving. The small amount of oil adds more flavor to foods when cooked in a heatproof oven bag.

3 1/2 cups packaged, raw cole slaw (Do not use "Angel Hair" type. If packaged slaw not available, use cabbage, sliced thin)
1 (15-ounce) can julienne cut beets, drained and rinsed
2 tablespoons water
2 teaspoons vegetable oil

Place slaw, beets, water and oil in a **heatproof oven bag**. Toss gently to combine. Tie and vent according to package directions and place in a **microwave**-safe casserole.
* Microwave at high temperature for about 5 minutes. (Rotate oven bag 1/2 turn halfway through cooking time if microwave does not have a carousel.) Rest 5 minutes.

2 tablespoons low-sodium soy sauce
1/8 teaspoon pepper
1/2 cup canned water chestnuts, sliced, drained and rinsed

Untie oven bag and add remaining ingredients. Toss gently to combine.

Use one of the alternate methods if your heatproof oven bag requires the use of flour.

27% calories from fat per serving

Yield: 6 servings

Nutrient content per serving:

Calories: 60   Fat: 1.8 g   Protein: 1.5 g   Carbohydrate: 9.4 g
Sodium: 413.8 mg   Cholesterol: 0.0 mg   Fiber: 2.3 g

Alternate Methods:

Microwave in a casserole: Combine slaw through oil in a plastic food storage bag. Toss to combine. Pour into a microwave-safe casserole. Cover tightly. Continue as * above.

Steam on stove: Place slaw and 1/2 cup water in a saucepan. Bring to a simmer, cover and cook for 5 to 10 minutes or until cabbage is just tender. Add beets during the last few minutes of cooking. Drain. Add oil through water chestnuts and toss.

Spinach with Rice and Dill

An adaptation of a Middle Eastern favorite, healthy and light.

1 pound frozen chopped spinach, loose-packed
1/4 cup long-grain white rice
1 1/4 cups water
1 tablespoon lemon juice
1/2 teaspoon dried dill weed
1/2 teaspoon salt

Spray **rice cooker** bowl with nonstick cooking spray and combine all ingredients. Turn on rice cooker and cook for 20 to 25 minutes or until the water is nearly absorbed and the rice is tender. Turn machine off and/or unplug. Let mixture sit for 5 minutes. Toss gently.

"Loose-packed" spinach is available in 1-pound plastic bags in the freezer section of the supermarket.

3% calories from fat per serving

Yield: 4 servings
Nutrient content per serving:
Calories: 83   Fat: 0.3 g   Protein: 4.4 g   Carbohydrate: 15.6 g
Sodium: 390.8 mg   Cholesterol: 0.0 mg   Fiber: 3.6 g

Alternate Method: Combine all ingredients in a saucepan, reduce water to 1 cup. Bring mixture to a boil, reduce heat, cover and simmer for 15 to 20 minutes or until water is nearly absorbed and rice is tender. Let sit for 5 minutes. Toss gently.

Pureed Carrots with Ginger

So low in fat, so high in vitamin A (2393 RE units per serving) and beta carotene (2407 Ug per serving) and so pretty.

3/4 pound baby carrots (for ease, buy prewashed and peeled), cut into 1-inch pieces
1 cup water
2 green onions, chopped
1/4 cup plain nonfat yogurt
1 tablespoon brown sugar
1/4 teaspoon ground ginger
1/4 teaspoon salt

Place carrots and water in a **microwave**-safe bowl. Cover tightly. Cook on high setting for 15 minutes or until carrots are very tender. (Rotate bowl 1/2 turn halfway through cooking time if microwave does not have a carousel.) Rest for 5 minutes. * Drain. Puree in a food processor along with the onions. (Or puree small batches in a blender.) Add remaining ingredients and process again quickly to combine. If not serving immediately, warm carefully for 2 minutes at medium temperature (50%) in the microwave. (If heated too quickly, yogurt may separate and appear "curdled".)

3% calories from fat per serving

Yield: 4 servings
Nutrient content per serving:
Calories: 63   Fat: 0.2 g   Protein: 1.7 g   Carbohydrate: 13.5 g
Sodium: 190.6 mg   Cholesterol: 0.6 mg   Fiber: 2.6 g

Alternate Method: Place carrots and water in a saucepan. Bring to a boil, reduce to a simmer, cover and cook for about 20 minutes or until carrots are very tender. Continue as * above. If desired, reheat over very low heat in the saucepan, stirring.

Broccoli with Sesame Seeds and Soy

1 pound broccoli flowerets
1 tablespoon low-sodium soy sauce
1 tablespoon lemon juice
1 teaspoon vegetable oil
1 teaspoon sesame seeds
1/4 teaspoon ground ginger
1 garlic clove, minced

Toss and cook the broccoli with the seasonings in the heatproof oven bag with absolutely no cleanup. Think stir-fry with almost no oil. This dish is a very good source of vitamin C containing 106 mg per serving.

Place all ingredients in a **heatproof oven bag**. Toss gently to combine. Tie and vent according to package directions and place in a **microwave-safe casserole**. Microwave at high temperature for about 4 minutes for tender-crisp broccoli or 7 minutes for a more tender broccoli. * (If microwave does not have a carousel, rotate casserole 1/2 turn halfway through cooking time.) Rest 5 minutes. Carefully toss again.

Use one of the alternate methods if your heatproof oven bag requires the use of flour.

26% calories from fat per serving

Yield: 4 servings
Nutrient content per serving:
Calories: 56   Fat: 1.6 g   Protein: 3.6 g   Carbohydrate: 6.7 g
Sodium: 467.2 mg   Cholesterol: 0.0 mg   Fiber: 3.5 g

Alternate Methods:
Microwave in a casserole: Combine ingredients in a plastic food storage bag. Toss to combine. Transfer to a microwave-safe casserole. Cover tightly. Cook at high for 4 to 7 minutes or until done to taste. Continue as * above.

Steam on stove: Place broccoli and garlic in a steamer basket over 1 inch of boiling water in a large saucepan. Cover. Steam for about 8 to 10 minutes or until just tender. Transfer broccoli and garlic to a serving bowl and add remaining ingredients. Toss gently.

Zucchini with Garlic and Oregano

Using a heatproof oven bag in the microwave produces a tender-crisp taste not unlike steaming in a basket. But the seasoning is in the bag, and the flavor is more intense!

2 pounds (6-inch long) zucchini squash
2 garlic cloves, minced
1 teaspoon dried oregano leaves
3/4 teaspoon salt
1 teaspoon vegetable oil
1 tablespoon chicken broth or water

* Scrub squash. Trim ends. Cut into 2-inch pieces. If squash is 1 inch in diameter, halve each piece; if larger, quarter each piece. Place all ingredients in a **heatproof oven bag**. Toss to combine. Tie and vent according to package directions and place in a **microwave**-safe casserole. Microwave at high temperature for 5 to 10 minutes depending on taste - 5 minutes for very crisp zucchini, 10 minutes for a more tender zucchini. ** (If microwave does not have a carousel, rotate casserole 1/2 turn halfway through cooking time.) Rest 5 minutes. Carefully toss again.

Use one of the alternate methods if your heatproof oven bag requires the use of flour.

23% calories from fat per serving

Yield: 6 servings
Nutrient content per serving:
Calories: 35   Fat: 0.9 g   Protein: 1.0 g   Carbohydrate: 5.6 g
Sodium: 294.4 mg   Cholesterol: 0.0 mg   Fiber: 0.1 g

Alternate Methods:
Microwave in a casserole: Prepare squash as * above and toss with remaining ingredients in a plastic food storage bag. Transfer to a microwave-safe casserole. Cover tightly. Cook on high for 5 to 10 minutes or until done to taste. Continue as ** above.

Steam on stove: Place zucchini and garlic in a steamer basket over 1 inch of boiling water in a large saucepan. Cover. Steam for about 8 to 10 minutes or until just tender. Transfer zucchini and garlic to a serving bowl and add remaining ingredients. Toss gently.

Seasoned Corn on the Cob

Experiment with your favorite herbs and spices. They permeate the corn when they're wrapped and cooked in the microwave.

2 teaspoons margarine, melted
1/2 teaspoon curry powder
2 tablespoons fresh parsley, minced
1/2 teaspoon salt
4 medium-sized ears of corn

* Combine margarine through salt in a small bowl. Remove husks and silk from corn and wash. Cut 4 (12-inch) long pieces of waxed paper. Place each ear in center of each piece. Brush with margarine mixture. Roll paper around corn and fold ends under to seal. Arrange in a circle in a large, **microwave**-safe platter. Microwave at high temperature for about 12 minutes. (Rotate platter 1/2 turn halfway through cooking time if microwave does not have a carousel.) Rest 5 minutes.

Use vegetable or olive oil instead of margarine if desired. Try dried basil leaves instead of curry powder for a totally different treat.

24% calories from fat per serving

Yield: 4 servings
Nutrient content per serving:
Calories: 103   Fat: 2.8 g   Protein: 2.3 g   Carbohydrate: 17.2 g
Sodium: 325.3 mg   Cholesterol: 0.0 mg   Fiber: 0.1 g

Alternate Method: Prepare margarine mixture and corn as * above. Cook corn in kettle of boiling water for 5 to 10 minutes or until tender. Drain on paper towels. Brush with margarine mixture.

Minted Grilled Red Onions

These tasty, attractive onions can be prepared in advance and reheated.

3 red onions (about 2 1/2 pounds), peeled and sliced crosswise 1/2-inch thick
2 tablespoons water

* Insert 2 toothpicks horizontally through each onion slice in order to prevent it from falling apart. Place onions and water in a **microwave**-safe casserole. Cover. Cook for 5 minutes or until onions are tender-crisp. (Rotate casserole 1/2 turn halfway through cooking time if microwave does not have a carousel.) Drain.

3 tablespoons red wine vinegar
1 tablespoon vegetable oil
1 tablespoon dried mint leaves
1 teaspoon sugar
1/2 teaspoon salt

** Meanwhile combine vinegar through salt in a heavy-duty zip-top plastic storage bag. Add onions, seal bag, turn to coat, and marinate, refrigerated, for several hours or overnight. Spray **grill** with nonstick cooking spray. Grill onions at medium-high heat for about 5 minutes on each side or until lightly browned and tender. Brush with marinade while grilling. If not serving immediately, place on a flat dish, cover, and refrigerate. At serving time, uncover, and microwave at high heat for 1 to 2 minutes or until just warmed. Remove toothpicks before serving.

24% calories from fat per serving

Yield: 6 servings
Nutrient content per serving:
Calories: 94   Fat: 2.5 g   Protein: 2.0 g   Carbohydrate: 15.8 g
Sodium: 198.7 mg   Cholesterol: 0.0 mg   Fiber: 0.0 g

Alternate Method: Prepare onions as * above. Boil in 2 quarts water for 5 minutes or until tender-crisp. Remove, dry and marinate as ** above. Spray a broiler pan with nonstick cooking spray. Broil onions at medium high about 6 inches from the heat for about 5 minutes on each side or until lightly browned and tender. Brush with marinade while broiling. Remove toothpicks.

Peppered Apples with Balsamic Vinegar

Pepper and balsamic vinegar intensify the taste of the apples. This is an excellent accompaniment to a grilled main dish.

4 Macintosh apples, cored, unpeeled and sliced 1/2-inch thick
1/2 teaspoon nutmeg
1/2 teaspoon cinnamon

* Spray apple slices lightly with nonstick cooking spray, butter flavored if possible. Dust with nutmeg and cinnamon. Spray **grill** with cooking spray. Grill apple slices at medium heat for about 3 minutes or until apples just begin to soften. Turn carefully and grill for 1 minute more or until they are just golden. ** Remove and halve each slice. Place in a serving bowl.

1/8 teaspoon white pepper
2 tablespoons balsamic vinegar

Dust with pepper and drizzle with vinegar. Toss gently.

6% calories from fat per serving

Yield: 4 servings
Nutrient content per serving:
Calories: 79   Fat: 0.5 g   Protein: 0.3 g   Carbohydrate: 18.3 g
Sodium: 0.8 mg   Cholesterol: 0.0 mg   Fiber: 3.2 g

Alternate Method: Spray a broiler pan with nonstick cooking spray. Prepare apples as * above. Broil apples at medium heat about 6 inches from the heat for about 5 minutes or until they begin to soften. Turn and broil for a couple of minutes more or until they are just golden. Continue as ** above.

Mapled Acorn Squash

This "hands free" recipe is only a starting point for your own ideas and tastes.

3 (1 1/2-pounds each) acorn squash, halved
6 tablespoons maple syrup
1/2 teaspoon salt
1/8 teaspoon pepper

* Preheat oven to 325 degrees. Scrape out seeds from squash with a spoon and discard. Cut a thin slice from the bottom of each squash half to prevent wobbling. Place 1 tablespoon syrup in each squash cavity. Brush inside and cut edges with some of the syrup. Sprinkle each half with salt and pepper and place carefully in a **heatproof oven bag** in a baking pan. (If your heatproof oven bag requires the use of flour, refer to the Special notes on pages 14 and 15.) Tie and vent according to package directions. Bake for 45 minutes to 1 hour or until a sharp knife, cut through the oven bag, pierces the flesh easily. Slit the oven bag to remove the squash.

6 teaspoons lemon juice

** Add 1 teaspoon lemon juice to each cavity and fluff flesh with a fork.

1% calories from fat per serving

Yield: 6 servings
Nutrient content per serving:
Calories: 197   Fat: 0.3 g   Protein: 2.6 g   Carbohydrate: 46.0 g
Sodium: 204.8 mg   Cholesterol: 0.0 mg   Fiber: 0.0 g

Alternate Method: Preheat oven and prepare squash as * above. Spray a casserole large enough to hold 6 halves with nonstick cooking spray. Place squash in the casserole and bake for about 1 hour 15 minutes, basting frequently or until squash tests done. Continue from ** above.

Eggplant with Peppers, Onions and Sun-Dried Tomatoes

The heatproof oven bag produces a juicier eggplant with all the flavor intact since both moisture and flavor are trapped in the oven bag.

1 (1 1/4-pound) eggplant, ends trimmed, cut lengthwise into 4 pieces (do not peel)
1 tablespoon vegetable oil
1/2 teaspoon salt
1/8 teaspoon pepper
1 green pepper, cored, seeded, cut into 1/2-inch slices
1/2 onion, peeled, cut into 1/4-inch slices and divided into rings
12 sun dried tomatoes, not oil-packed, soaked 5 minutes in boiling water and then drained
1 teaspoon dried oregano leaves
4 teaspoons lemon juice

* Preheat oven to 375 degrees. Brush eggplant lightly with oil, then sprinkle with salt and pepper. Layer each slice with green pepper, onion and 3 tomatoes. Sprinkle with oregano and drizzle with lemon juice. Carefully, place eggplant in a **heatproof oven bag** in a baking pan. (If your heatproof oven bag requires the use of flour, refer to the Special notes on pages 14 and 15.) Tie and vent according to package directions. Bake for 40 minutes or until a finger pressed through the oven bag makes a dent in the eggplant. Slit oven bag to remove eggplant.

30% calories from fat per serving

Yield: 4 servings
Nutrient content per serving:
Calories: 121   Fat: 4.0 g   Protein: 2.6 g   Carbohydrate: 18.6 g
Sodium: 367.9 mg   Cholesterol: 0.0 mg   Fiber: 2.2 g

Alternate Method: Preheat oven to 375 degrees. Spray a casserole large enough to hold eggplant in one layer with nonstick cooking spray. Place eggplant in casserole and prepare as * above. Cover with foil. (Spray inside of foil with nonstick cooking spray to prevent foil from sticking to the vegetables.) Bake for about 45 minutes or until tender. Add 2 tablespoons water, if necessary, to keep casserole moist.

Baked Herbed Mushrooms

Even mushroom haters will love them prepared this way. Serve as an accompaniment to meat or with toothpicks as an appetizer.

flour
16 ounces whole mushrooms, washed, dried and stems trimmed
1 teaspoon olive oil
1 teaspoon dried thyme leaves
1/2 teaspoon garlic powder
1/2 teaspoon salt
dash pepper

Preheat oven to 400 degrees. Add the amount of flour to a **heatproof oven bag** according to package directions. Place all ingredients in the oven bag. Turn gently to cover mushrooms with oil and herbs. Tie and vent according to package directions. Place in a baking pan and bake for 15 minutes. * Toss again gently and serve with the gravy produced in the oven bag.

If your heatproof oven bag does not require the addition of flour, and you eliminate it, seasoned mushroom "juices" will result instead of gravy. The mushrooms and "juices" are especially delicious over green beans.

26% calories from fat per serving

Yield: 6 servings

Nutrient content per serving:

Calories: 27   Fat: 0.8 g   Protein: 1.9 g   Carbohydrate: 3.1 g
Sodium: 194.0 mg   Cholesterol: 0.0 mg   Fiber: 0.1 g

Alternate Method: Spray a casserole large enough to hold mushrooms in one layer with nonstick cooking spray. Toss mushrooms gently with remaining ingredients in a plastic food storage bag. Turn into the casserole and bake in preheated 400 degree oven, covered, for 10 minutes or until mushrooms begin to exude juices. Stir twice during this period. Uncover and cook for 5 to 10 minutes longer, stirring periodically, or until mushrooms are tender. Continue from * above.

Green Beans With Feta and Salsa

This is a spicy side dish which complements so many foods. Use mild, medium or hot salsa as desired to add just the right zest.

1 pound green beans, frozen or fresh (note: if fresh, trim ends; if frozen, use long, uncut)
1/4 cup water
2 tablespoons commercial fat-free Italian dressing
3 tablespoons feta cheese, finely crumbled
1/8 teaspoon pepper
1/2 cup commercial chunky salsa
2 tablespoons fresh cilantro or parsley, minced

Place frozen beans and water in a **microwave**-safe bowl, cover tightly and cook for a total of about 6 minutes, stirring after 3 minutes. (For fresh beans, cook about 4 minutes longer.) Rest for 5 minutes. * Refresh with cold water and dry well with paper towels. Toss beans carefully with salad dressing, feta and pepper in a heavy plastic storage bag. Spread tossed bean mixture evenly in a flat serving dish. Top with salsa and sprinkle with cilantro or parsley. Cover and refrigerate at least 4 hours. Bring to room temperature before serving.

30% calories from fat per serving

Yield: 6 servings
Nutrient content per serving:
Calories: 48   Fat: 1.6 g   Protein: 2.2 g   Carbohydrate: 6.1 g
Sodium: 287.4 mg   Cholesterol: 6.2 mg   Fiber: 2.9 g

Alternate Method: If using frozen beans, bring beans and 3/4 cup water to a boil in a saucepan. Reduce heat, cover, and simmer for about 6 minutes or until just tender. For fresh beans, cook for 20 to 30 minutes. Continue as * above.

Zucchini with Tomatoes and Onions

This is especially good when these vegetables are in season. Prepare up to one day in advance for the flavors to blend, then bring to room temperature to serve.

2 pounds medium zucchini squash, ends trimmed, diagonally sliced 1/2-inch thick
1 tablespoon vegetable oil
1 teaspoon dried oregano leaves

* Combine zucchini slices, oil and oregano in a heavy plastic storage bag and toss gently.

1 1/2 pounds tomatoes, trimmed, sliced 1/2-inch thick
1 medium onion, chopped
1 teaspoon dried oregano leaves, divided
1 teaspoon salt, divided
1/4 teaspoon pepper, divided
2 garlic cloves, minced

Layer half of zucchini, tomatoes and onions in a large **microwave**-safe casserole, about 2 inches deep, sprinkling the onion layer with 1/2 teaspoon oregano, 1/2 teaspoon salt, 1/8 teaspoon pepper and half of garlic. Repeat vegetable layers, again sprinkling onion layer with herbs. Cover tightly. Microwave at high temperature for 18 minutes or until vegetables are very tender. (Rotate casserole 1/2 turn halfway through cooking time if microwave does not have a carousel.) Rest 5 minutes. Baste with juices. ** Serve with a slotted spoon and drizzle with juices.

Eliminating the oil will reduce fat percentage to 7% (0.3 grams per serving). Let your tastebuds be your guide.

26% calories from fat per serving

Yield: 10 servings
Nutrient content per serving:
Calories: 58   Fat: 1.7 g   Protein: 1.5 g   Carbohydrate: 9.2 g
Sodium: 242.3 mg   Cholesterol: 0.0 mg   Fiber: 2.5 g

Alternate Method: Preheat oven to 350 degrees. Spray a large casserole, about 2 inches deep, with nonstick cooking spray. Prepare and layer vegetables as * above. Bake uncovered for 10 minutes, then cover and bake for about 1 1/4 hours or until vegetables are very tender. Baste with pan juices after about 1 hour of total cooking time. Serve as ** above.

Curried Cauliflower with Carrots

Once the cauliflower is cut into flowerets, the rest is a breeze. This dish can be prepared in advance and reheated.

1 (2-pound) head cauliflower, cored and cut into small flowerets
1/4 pound baby carrots (for ease, buy packaged, cleaned, peeled and washed), cut into 1-inch pieces
1 cup onion, chopped
2 garlic cloves, minced
1/2 cup chicken broth, defatted
1 tablespoon balsamic or red wine vinegar
1 teaspoon curry powder
1 teaspoon ground cumin
1/2 teaspoon salt

Place all ingredients in a **heatproof oven bag**. Toss gently to combine. Tie and vent according to package directions and place in a **microwave**-safe casserole. * Microwave at high temperature for about 10 minutes. (Rotate 1/2 turn halfway through cooking time if microwave does not have a carousel.) Rest 5 minutes. Toss again and serve.

Use one of the alternate methods if your heatproof oven bag requires the use of flour.

6% calories from fat per serving

Yield: 6 servings
Nutrient content per serving:
Calories: 61   Fat: 0.4 g   Protein: 3.4 g   Carbohydrate: 11.0 g
Sodium: 221.1 mg   Cholesterol: 0.0 mg   Fiber: 3.8 g

Alternate Methods:
Microwave in a casserole: Combine ingredients in a plastic food storage bag. Toss to combine. Pour into a microwave-safe casserole. Cover tightly. Continue from * above.

Steam on stove: Spray a large saucepan with nonstick cooking spray and cook onions until they begin to soften. Add remaining ingredients, except cauliflower, increasing amount of broth to 1 cup. Combine. Add cauliflower and toss to cover with broth mixture. Bring to a boil, reduce heat, and simmer, covered, stirring occasionally for about 15 minutes or until vegetables are tender. Toss and serve.

Whole Cauliflower with Yogurt Paprika Sauce

A pretty presentation: slice like a cake and enjoy.

1 (2-pound) head cauliflower
1/4 cup water

Remove leaves and core from cauliflower with a sharp knife. Slice off any discoloration on the white head. Place cauliflower and water in a **microwave**-safe casserole just large enough to hold it. Cover tightly. Cook at high temperature for about 9 minutes or until tender. (If microwave does not have a carousel, rotate casserole 1/2 turn halfway through cooking time.) Let rest 5 minutes.

1/2 teaspoon paprika
2 tablespoons parsley, minced

* Remove to a serving platter, sprinkle with paprika and parsley.

3/4 cup plain nonfat yogurt
3/4 teaspoon vegetable oil
3/4 teaspoon balsamic or red wine vinegar
1 1/2 teaspoons paprika
1/4 teaspoon salt
1/8 generous teaspoon cayenne pepper
1/8 generous teaspoon garlic powder

Meanwhile, combine yogurt through garlic powder in a glass bowl. Slice cauliflower into wedges and serve with the sauce.

12% calories from fat per serving

Yield: 6 servings
Nutrient content per serving:
Calories: 66   Fat: 0.9 g   Protein: 4.5 g   Carbohydrate: 10.0 g
Sodium: 178.4 mg   Cholesterol: 1.3 mg   Fiber: 0.2 g

Alternate Method: Set a vegetable steamer large enough to hold the head of cauliflower in a pot of boiling water. Place the cauliflower in the steamer, cover and cook for 15 to 20 minutes or until tender. Continue as * above.

Roasted Onions and Peppers With Rosemary

This savory accent to a grilled entree can be served warm or at room temperature.

1 1/2 tablespoons vegetable oil
3 tablespoons balsamic or red wine vinegar
1 teaspoon dried rosemary leaves
1/4 teaspoon crushed red pepper
1/2 teaspoon sugar
1 teaspoon salt
3 medium white onions, trimmed and quartered
2 green peppers, each cored, seeded and cut into 8 pieces

Preheat oven to 350 degrees. Combine oil through salt in a **heatproof oven bag**. Add onions and peppers. Toss gently so onions and peppers are covered with herb mixture. (If your heatproof oven bag requires the use of flour, refer to the Special notes on pages 14 and 15.) Tie and vent oven bag according to package directions and place in a baking pan. Bake for 45 minutes to 1 hour or until onions are very tender and light golden. Pierce an onion through the oven bag to test. Slit the bag to remove vegetables and juices.

This is also a delicious filling for a "veggie" sandwich.

28% calories from fat per serving

Yield: 8 servings
Nutrient content per serving:
Calories: 94   Fat: 2.9 g   Protein: 2.0 g   Carbohydrate: 14.9 g
Sodium: 295.7 mg   Cholesterol: 0.0 mg   Fiber: 1.0 g

Alternate Method: Preheat oven to 350 degrees. Spray a casserole with nonstick cooking spray. Combine oil through salt in a plastic food storage bag. Add 1/4 cup water. Add onions and peppers and toss gently. Turn into the casserole, cover and bake for 45 minutes to 1 hour, basting every 15 minutes, or until onions are very tender and light golden. Add more liquid if necessary.

Sweet Potato Wedges

A delightful way to eat the much neglected sweet potato; don't save this nutritious treat for the holidays. It's very high in vitamin A with 3035 RE units per serving.

4 large sweet potatoes or yams (about 3 pounds), scrubbed, dried, unpeeled and each cut into 6 long wedges
1 1/2 tablespoons vegetable oil
1/2 teaspoon cardamom (or nutmeg) powder
1 teaspoon paprika
1 teaspoon salt
1/8 teaspoon pepper
Optional: 1 tablespoon orange-flavored liqueur

Preheat oven to 375 degrees. Combine oil through pepper (and optional liqueur) in a **heatproof oven bag**. Add potatoes. Toss gently to cover potatoes with spice mixture. Let stand for at least 5 minutes for spices to moisten evenly. Toss again. (If your heatproof oven bag requires the use of flour, refer to the Special notes on pages 14 and 15.) Tie and vent according to package directions and place oven bag in a baking pan. Potatoes should be spread out as much as possible. Bake for 45 minutes to 1 hour or until potatoes are lightly browned and tender. Test potato by piercing through oven bag with a sharp knife. It should be tender but not mushy.

16% calories from fat per serving

Yield: 6 servings
Nutrient content per serving:
Calories: 225   Fat: 4.0 g   Protein: 3.0 g   Carbohydrate: 44.2 g
Sodium: 410.4 mg   Cholesterol: 0.0 mg   Fiber: 0.1 g

Alternate Method: Preheat oven to 375 degrees. Combine oil through pepper (and optional liqueur) in a plastic food storage bag. Add potatoes and toss gently. Let stand for at least 5 minutes for spices to moisten evenly. Toss again. Turn potatoes onto a baking sheet which has been coated with nonstick cooking spray. Bake for 45 minutes to 1 hour or until browned and tender, turning potatoes periodically so all sides brown evenly.

Roasted Artichokes

Roast artichokes in the heatproof oven bag with the seasonings and there's no need to "dip" into calorie-laden sauces.

2 large (12-ounce each) or 3 small (8-ounce each) globe artichokes, stems removed and tough outer leaves snapped off
2 tablespoons lemon juice
1/4 cup chicken broth, defatted
1 teaspoon vegetable oil
2 garlic cloves, minced
3/4 teaspoon dried thyme leaves
1/2 teaspoon salt
1/8 teaspoon pepper

Preheat oven to 325 degrees. * Cut off 1 inch from the top of each artichoke and discard. Using a sharp knife, halve artichokes from top to bottom. If large, cut each half into thirds; if small, halve each half (again from top to bottom). Cut out choke (the hairy center) from each segment and discard. (During preparation, drop each piece into a bowl of water with a little lemon juice added to prevent discoloration.) Combine lemon juice through pepper in a **heatproof oven bag**. Add artichokes. Toss gently to cover with herb mixture. (If your heatproof oven bag requires the use of flour, refer to the Special notes on pages 14 and 15.) Tie and vent oven bag according to package directions and place in a baking pan. Bake for 45 minutes or until artichokes are lightly browned and a sharp knife pierced through the oven bag into the meaty part (the heart) of the artichoke tests very tender. Slit the oven bag to remove artichokes and juices.

To enjoy this vegetable, scrape the flesh off the leaves with your teeth. Then discard the leaf and work your way to the wholly edible heart!

21% calories from fat per serving

Yield: *4 servings*

Nutrient content per serving:

Calories: 55   Fat: 1.3 g   Protein: 2.6 g   Carbohydrate: 8.1 g

Sodium: 349.2 mg   Cholesterol: 0.0 mg   Fiber: 0.1 g

Alternate Method: Preheat oven to 350 degrees. Prepare artichokes as * above. Combine lemon juice through pepper in a plastic food storage bag. Increase chicken broth to 1/2 cup. Add artichokes and toss gently to cover with herb mixture. Transfer artichokes and liquid to a nonaluminun casserole. Bring to a boil, then bake, covered, for 45 minutes or until the heart tests very tender. Turn and baste every 15 minutes. Add more liquid if necessary.

Baked Sweet Potatoes

You don't need a cookbook for this recipe; but for those who've never tried sweet potatoes in the microwave - this is for you.

**6 medium sweet potatoes or yams
(about 3 pounds)
3/4 cup plain nonfat yogurt
1/4 teaspoon nutmeg**

Scrub and dry potatoes. Pierce skin to allow steam to escape. Arrange in a circle on a large **microwave**-safe platter. Cook at high for about 9 minutes or until a fork punctures potatoes easily. (Rotate 1/2 turn halfway through cooking time if microwave does not have a carousel.) Rest 5 minutes. * Slash top and fluff potatoes with a fork. Add 2 tablespoons yogurt to each potato and dust with nutmeg.

For 2 potatoes, cook about 6 minutes; for 4 potatoes, cook about 8 minutes. Sweet potatoes are high in both vitamin A (3014 RE units per serving) and vitamin C (30 mg per serving).

3% calories from fat per serving

Yield: 6 servings
Nutrient content per serving:
Calories: 206   Fat: 0.6 g   Protein: 4.5 g   Carbohydrate: 45.6 g
Sodium: 46.3 mg   Cholesterol: 1.3 mg   Fiber: 0.0 g

Alternate Method: Preheat oven to 375 degrees. Bake for about 45 minutes or until potatoes test done. Continue as * above.

Roast Potatoes with Oregano

No other technique for roasting potatoes can compare for ease, taste and reduced amount of oil required; this is one of our favorites!

2 tablespoons vegetable oil
1 teaspoon dried oregano leaves
1 teaspoon paprika
1 teaspoon salt
1/8 teaspoon pepper

Preheat oven to 375 degrees. Combine oil through pepper in a **heatproof oven bag**.

6 medium baking potatoes (about 2 1/2 pounds), scrubbed, unpeeled and each cut into 6 long wedges

Add potatoes. Toss gently to cover potatoes with herb mixture. Let potatoes sit for at least 5 minutes for herbs to moisten potatoes evenly. Toss again. (If your heatproof oven bag requires the use of flour, refer to the Special notes on pages 14 and 15.) Tie and vent oven bag according to package directions and place in a baking pan. Potatoes should be spread out as much as possible. Bake for about 1 hour or until lightly browned and tender. Test potato by piercing through oven bag with a sharp knife. It should be tender but not mushy.

15% calories from fat per serving

Yield: 8 servings
Nutrient content per serving:
Calories: 222   Fat: 3.6 g   Protein: 4.0 g   Carbohydrate: 43.3 g
Sodium: 304.4 mg   Cholesterol: 0.0 mg   Fiber: 4.2 g

Alternate Method: Preheat oven to 375 degrees. Combine oil through pepper in a plastic food storage bag. Add potatoes and toss gently. Let stand for at least 5 minutes for herbs to moisten evenly. Toss again. Turn potatoes onto a baking sheet which has been coated with nonstick cooking spray. Bake for about 1 hour or until browned and tender, turning potatoes periodically so all sides brown evenly.

Herbed Potato Packets

Packaged with loads of herbs and garlic; prepare the packets in advance, then cook them at the last minute.

8 baking potatoes (about 3 pounds, total), peeled and cut into 1-inch pieces
3 tablespoons vegetable oil
1 1/2 teaspoons dried basil leaves
1 1/2 teaspoons chives (fresh or frozen)
1 1/2 teaspoons dried thyme leaves
5 garlic cloves, minced
1 1/4 teaspoons salt
1/4 teaspoon pepper

* Toss all ingredients in a heavy plastic storage bag. Cut heavy-duty aluminum foil into 4 long pieces. (Or cut regular foil into 8 pieces, then double.) Divide and mound potatoes on foil. Wrap securely by folding long edges together first (about 3 turns), then short edges (again, about 3 turns). **Grill** at medium high for about 25 minutes, turning once or twice. (If packets have been prepared in advance and refrigerated, grill for 35 minutes.) Unwrap carefully and transfer contents to a serving bowl.

22% calories from fat per serving

Yield: 8 servings
Nutrient content per serving:
Calories: 221   Fat: 5.4 g   Protein: 3.7 g   Carbohydrate: 39.4 g
Sodium: 372.9 mg   Cholesterol: 0.0 mg   Fiber: 0.2 g

Alternate Method: Preheat oven to 450 degrees. Prepare packets as * above. Place packets on a cookie sheet and bake for about 30 minutes, turning once or twice.

Side Dishes
Rice, Beans, Grains, and Pasta

Simply Tomatoes and Rice

A simple, nearly fat-free rice side dish complements almost any main course.

1 (14 1/2-ounce) can stewed
  tomatoes
1 cup long-grain white rice
1 cup onion, minced
2 teaspoons paprika
1 teaspoon dried basil leaves
1/2 teaspoon salt
1/8 teaspoon pepper

Drain tomatoes and add water to drained liquid to measure 2 1/2 cups. Spray **rice cooker** container with non-stick cooking spray. Combine all ingredients with the liquid in the rice cooker, cover, turn on machine and cook for 25 to 30 minutes or until liquid is nearly absorbed. Turn off machine and/or unplug. * Let rice sit for 5 minutes. Fluff with a fork before serving.

2% calories from fat per serving

Yield: 6 servings
Nutrient content per serving:
Calories: 146   Fat: 0.3 g   Protein: 3.1 g   Carbohydrate: 32.7 g
Sodium: 326.4 mg   Cholesterol: 0.0 mg   Fiber: 1.6 g

Alternate Method: Drain tomatoes and add water to drained liquid to measure 2 1/2 cups liquid. Spray a saucepan with nonstick cooking spray. Combine all ingredients with the liquid in saucepan, bring to a boil, reduce heat, cover and simmer for 20 to 25 minutes or until liquid is nearly absorbed. Continue as * above.

Almost Mideast Pilaf

The difference between this and the real thing is about a stick of butter! This low-fat version is still a treat.

1 cup nested angel hair pasta, crumbled
1 tablespoon olive oil
1 cup long-grain white rice
2 1/2 cups chicken broth, defatted
1 teaspoon salt
1/4 teaspoon saffron or turmeric powder

Place pasta and oil in a **microwave**-safe dish. Microwave at high temperature for 1 minute, stirring after 30 seconds, until pasta is golden. Spray **rice cooker** container with nonstick cooking spray. Transfer pasta mixture to rice cooker. Add rice and stir to combine. Add broth and seasonings. Cover and cook for 25 to 30 minutes until water is nearly absorbed. Turn off machine and/or unplug. * Let rice sit for 5 minutes. Fluff with fork before serving.

13% calories from fat per serving

Yield: 6 servings

Nutrient content per serving:

Calories: 178   Fat: 2.6 g   Protein: 5.8 g   Carbohydrate: 32.9 g

Sodium: 395.0 mg   Cholesterol: 0.0 mg   Fiber: 0.8 g

Alternate Method: Spray a saucepan with nonstick cooking spray. Add oil and pasta and cook pasta, stirring, until it is just golden. Add rice and stir to combine. Add broth and seasonings. Bring to a boil, reduce heat, cover and simmer for 20 to 25 minutes or until water is nearly absorbed. Continue as * above.

Rice and Black Beans With Tomatoes and Green Chilies

Use stewed tomatoes instead of tomatoes and green chilies (if taste buds are fragile) in this almost fat-free rice.

1 (16-ounce) can diced tomatoes and green chilies
2 cups instant brown rice
1 (15 1/2-ounce) can black beans, drained and rinsed
1 teaspoon dried coriander leaves
1/2 teaspoon salt

Drain tomatoes and add water to drained liquid to measure 2 cups. Spray **rice cooker** container with nonstick cooking spray. Combine all ingredients with the liquid in the rice cooker, cover, turn on machine, and cook for 20 to 25 minutes or until liquid is nearly absorbed. Turn off machine and/or unplug. * Let sit 5 minutes. Fluff with a fork before serving.

Substitute any bean for the black bean.

7% calories from fat per serving

Yield: 6 servings
Nutrient content per serving:
Calories: 196   Fat: 1.6 g   Protein: 6.5 g   Carbohydrate: 38.8 g
Sodium: 565.2 mg   Cholesterol: 0.0 mg   Fiber: 5.5 g

Alternate Method: Drain tomatoes and add water to drained liquid to measure 2 cups. Spray a saucepan with nonstick cooking spray. Combine all ingredients with the liquid in saucepan. Bring to a boil, reduce heat, cover and simmer for 15 to 20 minutes or until liquid is nearly absorbed. Continue as * above.

Lentils in Chunky Tomato Sauce

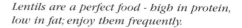

Lentils are a perfect food - high in protein, low in fat; enjoy them frequently.

1 (14 1/2-ounce) can diced tomatoes
1 cup dried brown lentils
1 cup onion, chopped
1 garlic clove, minced
1 tablespoon vegetable oil
2 tablespoons lemon juice
1/2 teaspoon salt
dash cayenne pepper

Drain tomatoes and add water to drained liquid to measure 2 cups liquid. Spray **rice cooker** container with non-stick cooking spray. Combine all ingredients with the liquid in the rice cooker. Cover. Cook for 30 minutes or until lentils are tender but not mushy. Turn machine off and/or unplug. Stir before serving.

15% calories from fat per serving

Yield: 6 servings

Nutrient content per serving:

Calories: 160   Fat: 2.6 g   Protein: 9.9 g   Carbohydrate: 24.2 g
Sodium: 315.7 mg   Cholesterol: 0.0 mg   Fiber: 10.9 g

Alternate Method: Drain tomatoes and add water to drained liquid to measure 2 cups liquid. Combine all ingredients with the liquid in a saucepan. Bring to a boil, reduce to a simmer and cook, covered, for 30 minutes or until lentils are tender.

Pinto Beans with Spinach

High in fiber, protein, iron (5 mg) and low in fat, this is a healthy one-dish meal!

2 cups dried pinto beans
2 cups chicken broth, defatted
2 cups water
1 teaspoon salt
1 teaspoon dried thyme leaves
1 bay leaf

Soak beans in water to cover overnight. Drain. Place in the **slow cooker** along with broth through bay leaf. Cover and cook at high temperature for 3 1/2 to 4 hours or until beans are tender but not mushy. * Drain beans in a colander set over a bowl, reserving the liquid. Discard the bay leaf. Puree 1 1/2 cups drained beans with 1 cup of the liquid in a food processor. (Or puree small batches in a blender.) Reserve remaining liquid.

1 cup onion, chopped
10 ounces fresh spinach (if possible, purchase pre-washed and trimmed), torn coarsely into pieces
1/4 cup water

Place onions in a large **microwave-**safe bowl with 1/4 cup water. Top with spinach. Cover bowl tightly. Microwave at high setting for 6 minutes or until spinach is wilted. (Rotate bowl 1/2 turn halfway through cooking time if microwave does not have a carousel.)

2 tablespoons lemon juice
1/2 teaspoon dried dill weed
1/4 teaspoon pepper

Return puree and remaining beans to the slow cooker along with the spinach, onions, and remaining ingredients. Combine, cover, and cook at high setting for 45 minutes to 1 hour or until beans are tender. Add reserved liquid, if necessary, to thin.

3% calories from fat per serving

Yield: 8 servings
Nutrient content per serving:
Calories: 194   Fat: 0.7 g   Protein: 12.9 g   Carbohydrate: 34.0 g
Sodium: 330.3 mg   Cholesterol: 0.0 mg   Fiber: 13.2 g

Alternate Method: Soak beans overnight and drain. Place beans through bay leaf in a large Dutch oven. Bring to a boil, reduce to a simmer and cook, covered, for 1 1/4 hours or until beans are tender but not mushy. (Add more water, if necessary, during this cooking period.) Drain and puree beans as * above. Meanwhile, spray a saucepan with nonstick cooking spray and saute onions for 4 to 5 minutes until softened. Add spinach and 1/4 cup water, cover and simmer for 3 to 4 minutes until wilted. Return puree and remaining beans to the Dutch oven along with spinach, onions and remaining ingredients. Combine, cover and simmer for another 30 minutes until beans are tender. Add reserved liquid if necessary.

Mexi~Corn and Black Beans

Use just 1 tablespoon chili powder and 1/4 teaspoon pepper for less "punch" in this oh-so-easy dish.

1 (10-ounce) package frozen corn
1/2 cup onion, minced
2 garlic cloves, minced
1/4 cup chicken broth, defatted
1 (15-ounce) can black beans,
  drained and rinsed
1 1/2 tablespoons chili powder
1/2 teaspoon salt
1/2 teaspoon pepper

Place frozen corn in its package on a paper plate in the **microwave**. Cook at high temperature for 5 minutes. (Rotate package 1/2 turn halfway through cooking time if microwave does not have a carousel.) Rest for 5 minutes. Meanwhile, place onion and garlic in a microwave-safe casserole along with chicken broth. Cover and cook at high temperature for 3 minutes. Add corn, beans and seasonings to onion mixture, cover and microwave at high temperature for 5 minutes more.

7% calories from fat per serving

Yield: 6 servings

Nutrient content per serving:

Calories: 130   Fat: 1.0 g   Protein: 6.5 g   Carbohydrate: 23.8 g
Sodium: 450.9 mg   Cholesterol: 0.0 mg   Fiber: 6.4 g

Alternate Method: Spray a saucepan with nonstick cooking spray. Saute onions and garlic until softened. Add corn and broth, bring to a boil, reduce to a simmer, cover and cook for about 3 minutes. Add remaining ingredients, cover and cook for about 5 minutes more.

Boston Baked Beans

Once you use this slow cooker technique to cook beans, you'll be forever spoiled. Since there's no soaking, cooking time is long. The key word here is "easy"!

1 (16-ounce) package dried small white beans
6 cups water
1 cup thinly sliced onions
3 tablespoons dark molasses
3 tablespoons Dijon mustard
1/4 cup brown sugar, packed
2 cloves garlic, minced
2 teaspoons smoked salt flavoring (if not available, use "liquid smoke")

Combine all ingredients in the **slow cooker**. Cover and cook on high for about 2 hours. Liquid will be hot but not simmering. Reduce temperature to low and cook for 18 to 20 hours or until beans are very tender and nicely browned. (Take a quick peek now and then; add a little boiling water if beans appear dry.) Adjust seasoning to taste.

These beans are wonderful with "Rye Bread With Beer", page 50. Cooking time for beans can vary widely depending on the particular crop of beans.

4% calories from fat per serving

Yield: 15 (1/2-cup) servings

Nutrient content per serving:

Calories: 136   Fat: 0.6 g   Protein: 6.7 g   Carbohydrate: 26 g
Sodium: 199.9 mg   Cholesterol: 0.06 mg   Fiber: 0.3 g

Alternate Method: Soak beans in cold water at least 6 hours or overnight. Drain. Place beans in a large Dutch oven along with 8 cups water, bring to a boil, reduce to a simmer and cook, covered, for 30 to 45 minutes or until just tender. Drain again. Add onions through salt along with 2 cups boiling water or just enough to cover the beans. Bake, covered, in a preheated 300 degree oven for 4 to 6 hours or until beans are browned and very tender. Stir periodically. (Add a little boiling water if beans appear dry.)

Lima Beans with Tomato Sauce

Here's still another way to automatically have a nutritious, almost fat-free dish. Add a salad and an ear of corn, and you have a complete meal as beans are protein-packed.

1 pound (2 1/2 cups) dried lima beans

Soak beans in 6 cups water for at least 6 hours or overnight. Don't drain. Turn into a **slow cooker** and cook at low setting for 8 to 9 hours or until very tender. Drain.

1 (14 1/2-ounce) can tomatoes, chopped
1/2 teaspoon onion powder
1/2 teaspoon garlic powder
1 teaspoon chili powder
1 teaspoon dried oregano leaves, crushed
1 1/2 teaspoons salt
1/4 teaspoon black pepper

Add remaining ingredients to the beans and transfer mixture to a shallow **microwave**-safe casserole. Cover and microwave at high for about 15 minutes or until bubbling. (Rotate 1/2 turn halfway through cooking time if microwave does not have a carousel.) Rest for 5 minutes.

3% calories from fat per serving

Yield: 15 (1/2-cup) servings
Nutrient content per serving:
Calories: 100   Fat: 0.3 g   Protein: 5.3 g   Carbohydrate: 18.9 g
Sodium: 293.5 mg   Cholesterol: 0.0 mg   Fiber: 0.3 g

Alternate Method: Soak beans in 6 cups water for at least 6 hours or overnight. Drain beans and place in a large Dutch oven along with 1 1/2 quarts water. Bring to a boil, reduce to a simmer and cook, covered, for about 2 hours or until beans are tender. Drain. Combine with remaining ingredients and transfer to a shallow heatproof casserole. Bake, uncovered, in a preheated 350 degree oven for 45 minutes to 1 hour or until bubbling. Do not allow beans to become dry.

Bulgur Wheat "California"

The microwave produces a wonderful cooked bulgur. Use this healthy high protein grain frequently and experiment by adding 1 cup of your favorite cooked vegetables at the start of the reduced cooking temperature.

2 cups water
1 cup bulgur (cracked wheat),
  uncooked
2 tablespoons (1/2 package)
  dry onion soup mix

Place water in a **microwave**-safe casse-role. Microwave at high temperature, covered, for 5 minutes or just until it comes to a simmer. Add remaining ingredients, cover and cook at high for 3 minutes. Then cook at medium tem-perature (50%) for 5 minutes. (Rotate 1/2 turn halfway through cooking time if microwave does not have a carousel.)

Let rest a couple of minutes. Stir with a fork to fluff and combine.

If your grocer doesn't carry this grain, go to your local health food store, buy in bulk (medium-sized grain) and store refrigerated! Or use packaged taboule and save the enclosed seasoning pack for another use.

4% calories from fat per serving

Yield: 4 servings
Nutrient content per serving:
Calories: 150   Fat: 0.7 g   Protein: 4.4 g   Carbohydrate: 31.6 g
Sodium: 441.5 mg   Cholesterol: 0.2 mg   Fiber: 6.1 g

Alternate Method: Combine water, bulgur and dry soup in a saucepan. Bring to a boil, reduce to a simmer, cover and cook for 20 to 25 minutes or until water is nearly absorbed. Let rest 5 minutes. Stir with a fork.

Pasta with Tomato Sauce

This is a quick, fat-free tomato sauce which can be used where ever a spicy sauce is needed. Don't limit it to pasta!

1/2 cup onions, minced
1/4 cup white wine or chicken broth, defatted

Combine onions and wine in a 2-quart **microwave**-safe bowl. Microwave at high temperature, uncovered, for about 2 minutes or until onions are softened.

1 (14 1/2-ounce) can diced tomatoes
1 tablespoon tomato paste
1/2 teaspoon sugar
1 teaspoon dried basil leaves
1/2 teaspoon dried oregano leaves
1/4 teaspoon garlic powder
1/2 teaspoon salt
1/8 teaspoon pepper

Add remaining ingredients and microwave at high temperature, uncovered, for about 9 more minutes. (Rotate 1/2 turn halfway through cooking time if microwave does not have a carousel. Mixture will simmer for about 7 minutes.) Let sit for 5 minutes. Stir.

12 ounces pasta

* Toss sauce with pasta which has been cooked according to package directions.

Nutrient content does not include pasta.

3% calories from fat per serving

Yield: 6 servings
Nutrient content per serving:
Calories: 32   Fat: 0.1 g   Protein: 0.9 g   Carbohydrate: 5.4 g
Sodium: 338.1 mg   Cholesterol: 0.0 mg   Fiber: 1.0 g   Alcohol: .9 g

Alternate Method: Spray a saucepan with nonstick cooking spray. Brown onions over low heat until they are just softened. Add remaining ingredients and bring to a boil. Reduce heat to a simmer, cover and cook for about 10 minutes. Stir periodically. Continue from * above.

Pasta with Basil Sauce

A garlicky, light pasta dish; both easy and fast.

1 cup elbow macaroni
4 cups water

Cook and drain macaroni according to "Method for Cooking Pasta in the Microwave Using the **Heatproof Oven Bag**" on page 232.

1/4 cup chicken broth, defatted
1 1/2 teaspoons vegetable oil
1 garlic clove
3/4 teaspoon dried basil leaves
1/8 teaspoon red pepper flakes
1/4 teaspoon salt

Blend broth through salt in a food processor or a blender. Transfer to a **microwave**-safe bowl and microwave at high temperature for 1 minute. Toss with pasta.

17% calories from fat per serving

Yield: 4 servings
Nutrient content per serving:
Calories: 115   Fat: 2.1 g   Protein: 3.8 g   Carbohydrate: 20.1 g
Sodium: 155.8 mg   Cholesterol: 0.0 mg   Fiber: 0.7 g

Alternate Method: Cook macaroni according to package directions. Drain. Meanwhile blend broth through salt in a food processor or blender, transfer to a saucepan and heat gently until warmed. Toss with pasta.

Pasta with Meat Sauce

An old-fashioned meat sauce which is so right for today's Calorie and fat-conscious pasta lovers. Use this sauce when any recipe calls for a meat sauce.

1/2 pound fresh ground turkey
   breast
1/2 pound lean ground top round
1 1/2 cups onion, chopped
2 celery stalks, chopped
2 garlic cloves, minced
2 (1-pound) cans plum tomatoes
1 (6-ounce) can sodium-free tomato
   paste
1 (4-ounce) can mild jalapeño
   peppers, drained
1 tablespoon vegetable oil
1/4 cup red wine or beef broth,
   defatted
1/4 cup parsley, minced
1 tablespoon sugar
1 teaspoon dried basil leaves
1 teaspoon dried oregano leaves
1 1/2 teaspoons salt

2 pounds cooked pasta

Place meat in a **microwave**-safe dish. Cover. Cook on high, stirring after every 2 minutes, for about 5 minutes or until meat has just lost its pink color. Drain and pat dry with paper towels. Crumble meat into very small pieces with a wooden spoon. Drain tomatoes, reserving the juice. Coarsely chop tomatoes. Combine meat, tomatoes, drained tomato juice and remaining ingredients in a **slow cooker** and cook on low for 8 to 10 hours. (After 8 hours, tomatoes will still be slightly firm, after 10 hours, they will have mainly "melted" into the sauce.)

* Toss sauce with pasta which has been cooked according to package directions.

*To cut fat down to 13% per serving, use **all** fresh ground turkey breast. Nutrient content does not include pasta.*

18% calories from fat per serving

Yield: 10 servings
Nutrient content per serving:
Calories: 130   Fat: 2.6 g   Protein: 14.4 g   Carbohydrate: 11.3 g
Sodium: 747.7 mg   Cholesterol: 30.0 mg   Fiber: 2.1 g   Alcohol: .5 g

Alternate Method: Spray a large pot with nonstick cooking spray. Brown onion and garlic over low heat until onions are just softened. Add meat and cook, stirring, just until it loses its pink color. Drain juices and pat dry with paper towels. Add remaining ingredients, bring to a boil, reduce to a very low simmer and cook, covered, for about 2 hours. Stir periodically. Continue from * above.

Spaghettini with Grilled Zucchini and Onions

This lively taste treat can be served hot, warm or cold. The grilled vegetables are also good served alone.

3/4 pound spaghettini or vermicelli pasta
1 pound medium zucchini squash, ends trimmed and diagonally sliced 1/2-inch thick
1 medium onion, skin removed and sliced 1/2-inch thick
2 tablespoons water
4 teaspoons vegetable oil

Cook pasta according to package directions. Drain well and transfer to a large serving bowl. Meanwhile, place zucchini, onions and water in a **microwave**-safe casserole. Cover. Cook for about 6 minutes to partially cook the vegetables. (If microwave does not have a carousel, rotate 1/2 turn halfway through cooking time.) * Drain and dry. Toss vegetables in a heavy plastic storage bag with oil to coat. Spray a cooking tray or rack with small holes with nonstick cooking spray. (Use rack to prevent vegetables from falling through grill.) **Grill** vegetables at medium high heat for about 5 minutes on each side or until golden.

1/4 cup chicken broth, defatted
2 tablespoons vegetable oil
1 tablespoon lemon juice
1 teaspoon dried oregano leaves
1 teaspoon dried basil leaves
1/2 teaspoon red pepper flakes
1 teaspoon salt

** Combine broth through salt. Toss with pasta and vegetables.

25% calories from fat per serving

Yield: 6 servings
Nutrient content per serving:
Calories: 304   Fat: 8.6 g   Protein: 8.4 g   Carbohydrate: 48.3 g
Sodium: 396 mg   Cholesterol: 0.0 mg   Fiber: 3.0 g

Alternate Method: Boil vegetables in 2 quarts water for 5 minutes or until tender-crisp. Toss with oil as * above. Spray a broiler pan with nonstick cooking spray. Broil vegetables 6 to 7 inches from heat at medium heat for about 5 minutes on each side. Continue as ** above.

Baked Orzo in Tomato Sauce

Avoid both a messy pan and extra fat in this easy family favorite.

flour
3 1/2 cups water
1/2 cup low-sodium catsup
1 teaspoon Worcestershire sauce
1/2 teaspoon salt
1/8 teaspoon pepper
1 cup orzo (rice-shaped) pasta

Preheat oven to 400 degrees. Add the amount of flour to **heatproof oven bag** according to package directions. Combine water through pepper in the oven bag. Add orzo pasta. Squeeze to combine. Tie and vent oven bag according to package directions and place in a baking pan. Bake for 10 to 15 minutes or until liquid just begins to simmer. Reduce heat to 350 degrees and bake another 45 minutes or until liquid is nearly absorbed. (Mixture should not be totally dry.) Let stand for at least 5 minutes. Slit oven bag to serve pasta.

4% calories from fat per serving

Yield: 4 servings
Nutrient content per serving:
Calories: 196   Fat: 0.9 g   Protein: 5.8 g   Carbohydrate: 41.1 g
Sodium: 316.0 mg   Cholesterol: 0.0 mg   Fiber: 2.1 g

Alternate Method: Preheat oven to 350 degrees. Combine water through pepper in a saucepan and bring to a boil. Add orzo pasta, stirring. Transfer mixture to a baking pan which has been sprayed with nonstick cooking spray. Cover and bake for about 1 hour, stirring occasionally, until pasta is very tender and liquid is nearly absorbed. Remove from the oven and let stand for at least 5 minutes.

Couscous With Corn and Cumin

When you see the fat content and ease of preparation, it's hard to resist this pasta dish.

1 cup water
1/2 teaspoon ground cumin
1/4 teaspoon salt
2/3 cup dry packaged couscous

Place water, cumin and salt in a **microwave**-safe casserole. Cover and bring to a boil on high power in microwave, about 3 minutes. Add couscous. Stir. Cover and rest for 5 minutes.

1 cup frozen corn, loose-packed

Meanwhile, place corn in a small microwave-safe bowl, cover tightly and cook on high for 3 minutes or until just tender. Let stand 3 minutes.

(If microwave does not have a carousel, rotate 1/2 turn halfway through each cooking period.)

2 tablespoons minced, red onion

* Fluff couscous with a fork, add corn and onion, and combine.

"Loose-packed" corn is available in 1-pound plastic bags in the freezer section of the supermarket.

2% calories from fat per serving

Yield: 6 servings
Nutrient content per serving:
Calories: 102   Fat: 0.2 g   Protein: 3.5 g   Carbohydrate: 21.6 g
Sodium: 100.8 mg   Cholesterol: 0.0 mg   Fiber: 1.8 g

Alternate Method: Bring water, cumin and salt to a boil in a saucepan. Add couscous. Stir, cover and rest for 5 minutes. Cook corn according to package directions. Continue as * above.

Couscous with Artichoke Hearts

This unique technique yields a moister couscous as a result of the steaming effect of the heatproof oven bag.

flour
**1 (10-ounce) box couscous
(about 1 1/2 cups)**
2 1/4 cups chicken broth, defatted

Preheat oven to 325 degrees. Add the amount of flour to **heatproof oven bag** according to package directions. Pour couscous into the oven bag, add the broth and combine. Tie. Let stand 5 minutes.

**1 (14-ounce) can artichoke hearts,
drained and chopped into 1/2-inch
pieces**
2 tablespoons lemon juice
2 tablespoons vegetable oil
1 teaspoon dried basil leaves
1/2 teaspoon dried dill weed
1 teaspoon salt
1/8 teaspoon pepper

Meanwhile combine remaining ingredients and add to the couscous. Tie and vent oven bag according to package directions and place in a baking pan. (Tie near the end of the oven bag to leave expansion space.) Bake for 10 minutes or just until liquid is absorbed. Remove from the oven and let the couscous steam in the oven bag for 5 minutes more. Slit the oven bag to serve. Toss before serving.

This Moroccan pasta is a wonderful change of pace from the ordinary pastas, and it's so easy to prepare.

18% calories from fat per serving

Yield: 12 servings
Nutrient content per serving:
Calories: 121   Fat: 2.4 g   Protein: 4.8 g   Carbohydrate: 20.1 g
Sodium: 263.1 mg   Cholesterol: 0.0 mg   Fiber: 1.6 g

Alternate Method: Place all ingredients, except couscous and artichoke hearts, in a saucepan. Bring to a boil. Add couscous and stir. Cover. Remove from heat and let stand 5 minutes. Fluff lightly. Add artichoke hearts and combine.

Side Dishes
Salads

Notes

Mediterranean Pasta Salad

Use the heatproof oven bag to simplify your pasta-cooking, and enjoy this tasty pasta salad. Eliminate the olives if you wish, and fat content will be reduced to 4% along with a decrease in sodium content.

1 cup elbow macaroni
4 cups water

Cook macaroni according to "Method for Cooking Pasta in the **Microwave** Using the **Heatproof Oven Bag**" on page 232. Drain and rinse.

7 ounces canned artichoke hearts, water-packed, drained and rinsed, cut into 1/2-inch wedges
1 (7-ounce) jar sweet roasted red peppers, drained and cut into 1-inch pieces
4 green onions, including green tops, chopped
1/4 cup fresh parsley, minced
6 calamata olives, pitted and chopped (or ripe black olives)

* Place pasta in a large bowl and combine with artichokes through olives.

1/2 cup plus 2 tablespoons plain nonfat yogurt
1 tablespoon balsamic or red wine vinegar
1 tablespoon Dijon mustard
1 teaspoon dried basil leaves
1/2 teaspoon red pepper flakes
1/4 teaspoon garlic powder
1/2 teaspoon salt

Combine yogurt through salt. Toss gently with pasta mixture. Refrigerate, covered, at least 2 hours before serving to allow flavors to blend.

14% calories from fat per serving

Yield: 8 servings
Nutrient content per serving:
Calories: 93   Fat: 1.4 g   Protein: 3.6 g   Carbohydrate: 16.5 g
Sodium: 367.3 mg   Cholesterol: 0.8 mg   Fiber: 0.9 g

Alternate Method: Cook macaroni according to package directions. Drain and rinse. Continue as * above.

Eight Grains Plus One Salad

This is a high fiber, low-fat salad for the grain lovers.

1 cup "8-grain" mix (hard red
  winter wheat, long grain brown
  rice, whole oats, whole rye, whole
  triticale, whole barley, whole
  buckwheat and sesame seeds),
  uncooked
3 1/2 cups water
1/2 teaspoon salt
1/2 cup bulgur (cracked wheat),
  uncooked

3 tablespoons red onion, chopped
1/2 cup fresh minced parsley
1 tomato, diced
1/2 cup commercial fat-free Italian
  dressing
1/2 teaspoon salt
1/8 teaspoon pepper

Spray **rice cooker** container with non-stick cooking spray. Combine 8-grain mix through salt in rice cooker. Cover. Cook for about 30 minutes or until water is nearly absorbed. Add bulgur 20 minutes into cooking time. Turn machine off and/or unplug. * Let mixture rest, covered, for 5 minutes. Uncover and allow to cool before proceeding.

Add remaining ingredients and toss gently. Serve at room temperature.

Use packaged "taboule" and save the enclosed seasoning pack for another use if you can't find bulk bulgur wheat.

12% calories from fat per serving

Yield: 8 servings
Nutrient content per serving:
Calories: 131   Fat: 1.7 g   Protein: 4.3 g   Carbohydrate: 24.6 g
Sodium: 450.2 mg   Cholesterol: 0.0 mg   Fiber: 4.8 g

Alternate Method: Combine 8-grain mix, 3 cups water and salt in a saucepan. Bring to a boil, reduce to a simmer, cover and cook for about 25 minutes or until water is nearly absorbed. Add bulgur 15 minutes into cooking time and continue as * above.

Red Lentils and Bulgur Salad

An unusual combination results in a spicy (lentil), nutty (bulgur) flavor; also, high in fiber and low in fat.

3/4 cup dried red lentils
3/4 cup bulgur (cracked wheat), uncooked
2 cups water
1 teaspoon salt

Spray **rice cooker** container with nonstick cooking spray. Place lentils through salt in the rice cooker. Cook for 12 to 15 minutes or until water is nearly absorbed. Turn machine off and/or unplug. * Allow mixture to come to room temperature.

3 tablespoons red wine vinegar
1 tablespoon vegetable oil
1/4 cup chicken broth, defatted
1/3 cup red onion, chopped
1 cup frozen peas, thawed

Add vinegar, oil and broth and combine. Toss with onion and peas. Serve at room temperature.

Use packaged "taboule" and save the enclosed seasoning pack for another use if you can't find bulk bulgur wheat.

12% calories from fat per serving

Yield: 6 servings
Nutrient content per serving:
Calories: 205   Fat: 2.8 g   Protein: 10.4 g   Carbohydrate: 34.6 g
Sodium: 418.3 mg   Cholesterol: 0.0 mg   Fiber: 11.8 g

Alternate Method: Combine lentils through salt in a medium saucepan. Bring to a boil, reduce heat, cover and simmer for about 10 minutes or until water is nearly absorbed. Continue as * above.

Asparagus and Potato Salad

The microwave effectively "steams" the vegetables; no cleanup, no mess. Use the cooking plate again to serve this colorful salad.

1 pound asparagus spears
1 pound small round red potatoes,
cut, if necessary, to make them
approximately equal in size

* Snap off tough ends of asparagus. Cut into 2-inch diagonal pieces. Scrub potatoes and place in a circle around the edge of a 10-inch **microwave**-safe glass plate. Add 2 tablespoons water. Cover tightly. Cook on high for 4 minutes. Uncover carefully and place asparagus in the center of the dish. Cover tightly. Cook for 3 more minutes on high. (Rotate 1/2 turn halfway through both cooking times if microwave does not have a carousel.) Rest 5 minutes. ** Refresh potatoes and asparagus in cold water to stop cooking. Dry well in paper towels. Quarter potatoes. (If not serving immediately, keep wrapped in paper towels at room temperature.)

3/4 cup commercial fat-free Italian
dressing
1 tablespoon balsamic or red wine
vinegar
1/3 cup celery, finely minced
1/2 cup red onion, finely minced
1/4 cup parsley, minced

Combine dressing through parsley. Toss gently with asparagus and potatoes. If desired, serve on lettuce on individual salad plates.

This salad is at its best if not refrigerated. Cook vegetables hours ahead, then keep them at room temperature until tossing with remaining ingredients.

3% calories from fat per serving

Yield: 8 servings

Nutrient content per serving:

Calories: 79   Fat: 0.3 g   Protein: 2.4 g   Carbohydrate: 16.7 g

Sodium: 232.3 mg   Cholesterol: 0.0 mg   Fiber: 0.7 g

Alternate Method: Prepare vegetables as * above. Combine potatoes with enough cold water to cover them by 2 inches in a saucepan. Bring water to a boil and simmer, partially covered, for 15 to 20 minutes or until just tender. Boil asparagus, similarly, for about 5 minutes or until just tender. Continue as ** above.

Giant White Bean Salad

Try to find this wonderful giant bean; if unavailable, use a white kidney or navy bean.

1 cup dried giant white beans *2 1/2 cups water*	Place beans and water in the **slow cooker**. (Slow cooking will replace soaking.) Cook at low overnight and all day for a total of 18 to 20 hours or until the beans are very tender. Beans will brown.
1 cup frozen 1-inch cut green beans	Add green beans for an additional 30 minutes. * Drain. Allow beans to cool to room temperature.
1 tablespoon balsamic or red wine *vinegar* *1 tablespoon vegetable oil* *1 tablespoon lemon juice* *1/2 teaspoon salt* *1/2 teaspoon ground cumin* *1/8 teaspoon pepper* *1/2 cup minced fresh parsley* *1 cup tomato, diced*	Combine vinegar through pepper and toss with beans, parsley and tomato.

16% calories from fat per serving

Yield: 6 servings

Nutrient content per serving:

Calories: 147   Fat: 2.6 g   Protein: 8.2 g   Carbohydrate: 22.8 g

Sodium: 229.4 mg   Cholesterol: 0.0 mg   Fiber: 5.9 g

Alternate Method: Soak beans in water to cover overnight. Drain. Place beans and 2 1/2 cups water in a saucepan. Bring to a boil, reduce heat, cover and simmer for about 2 hours or until very tender. (Add more water, if necessary.) Cook green beans according to package directions. Continue as * above.

Tuna, Cannelini and Tomato Salad

Think about serving a warm salad so easy to assemble.

2 tablespoons Dijon mustard
1 tablespoon vegetable oil
2 garlic cloves, minced
2 tablespoons red onion, minced
1/2 teaspoon dried basil leaves
1/2 teaspoon salt
dash pepper
1 (3-ounce) can tuna, water-packed, drained
1 cup canned cannelini beans (or small white beans), drained and rinsed
2 tomatoes, each cut into 4 slices

* Combine mustard through pepper in a bowl. Add tuna and beans and toss. Place tomato slices in a flat **microwave**-safe dish large enough to hold them in one layer. Divide tuna mixture among the slices. Cover and cook at high temperature in the microwave for 4 minutes. (Rotate dish 1/2 turn halfway through cooking time if microwave does not have a carousel.)   Rest for 5 minutes. Serve warm.

For more pizazz, add pickled jalapeño pepper slices or minced green olives to the tuna mixture.

23% calories from fat per serving

Yield: 4 (2-slice) servings
Nutrient content per serving:
Calories: 174   Fat: 4.4 g   Protein: 12.3 g   Carbohydrate: 21.2 g
Sodium: 492.6 mg   Cholesterol: 6.5 mg   Fiber: 6.8 g

Alternate Method: Prepare tuna mixture and tomatoes as * above. Place in a heat-proof casserole which has been sprayed with nonstick cooking spray. Bake in a preheated 350 degree oven for about 15 minutes or until heated.

Grilled Leeks with Cucumber Sauce

This is an unusual salad using an often overlooked vegetable. Not planning to use the grill? Microwave the leeks until they are very tender, then continue from **, skipping the grill.

6 leeks, washed well
1 cup commercial fat-free Italian dressing

* Remove roots from leeks and cut tops where they become dark green. (About 7 inches will remain). Split leeks lengthwise. Wash again to remove all remaining dirt specks. Place in a **microwave**-safe dish in one layer, cut side down, add 1 tablespoon water, cover and cook at high temperature for about 7 minutes. (Rotate dish 1/2 turn halfway through cooking time if microwave does not have a carousel.) Rest 5 minutes. Leeks should be just tender. Drain water. Brush leeks on all sides with some of the dressing. Spray a **grill** rack with nonstick cooking spray. Grill leeks at medium heat for 3 to 5 minutes on each side or until they are golden. ** Transfer to a dish in one layer, pour remaining dressing over them and refrigerate until serving time. Before serving, bring leeks to room temperature.

2 ripe tomatoes, each cut into 6 slices
3/4 cup Cucumber Sauce (page 199)

Serve 2 leek halves over 2 tomato slices, and top with 2 tablespoons cucumber sauce.

Use a commercial fat-free creamy dressing instead of cucumber sauce for a time-saver.

5% calories from fat per serving

Yield: 6 servings

Nutrient content per serving:

Calories: 78   Fat: 0.4 g   Protein: 2.5 g   Carbohydrate: 16.1 g

Sodium: 451.1 mg   Cholesterol: 0.8 mg   Fiber: 4.5 g

Alternate Method: Prepare leeks as * above and steam in a vegetable steamer set over boiling water for 5 to 7 minutes or until just tender. Brush on all sides with some of the dressing. Spray a broiler pan with nonstick cooking spray. Place leeks on the pan and broil at medium heat 5 to 6 inches from the heat for 3 to 5 minutes on each side. Watch so they don't burn. Continue as ** above.

Rice Salad with Tomato and Cucumber

Prepare this salad a few hours in advance and refrigerate. It is also a delightful filling for hollowed-out tomatoes.

2/3 cup long-grain white rice
1 2/3 cups water
1 cup tomato, diced
1 cup peeled seeded cucumber, diced
1/2 cup fresh parsley, minced
1 teaspoon dried mint leaves, crumbled
1/2 teaspoon dried dill weed
1/2 teaspoon salt
3/4 cup Creamy Feta Dressing, page 205

Spray **rice cooker** container with non-stick cooking spray. Combine rice and water in rice cooker, cover and cook for 15 to 20 minutes or until water is nearly absorbed. Turn off machine and/or unplug. * Let rice sit for 5 minutes. Uncover and let rice come to room temperature. Combine rice with remaining ingredients up to dressing. Add dressing and toss gently.

16% calories from fat per serving

Yield: 6 servings
Nutrient content per serving:
Calories: 117   Fat: 2.1 g   Protein: 4.3 g   Carbohydrate: 20.3 g
Sodium: 500 mg   Cholesterol: 7.6 mg   Fiber: 1.2 g

Alternate Method: Spray a saucepan with nonstick cooking spray. Add rice and water, bring to a boil, reduce heat, cover and simmer for 10 to 15 minutes or until water is nearly absorbed. Continue as * above.

Marinades, Sauces, Dressings and Rubs

Marinades, Sauces, Dressings and Rubs

Curry Sauce

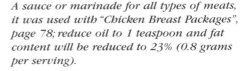

A sauce or marinade for all types of meats, it was used with "Chicken Breast Packages", page 78; reduce oil to 1 teaspoon and fat content will be reduced to 23% (0.8 grams per serving).

1/4 cup tomato sauce
1/3 cup white wine
1 tablespoon vegetable oil
1 tablespoon sugar
1 teaspoon curry powder
1 teaspoon Worcestershire sauce
1/2 teaspoon salt
1 garlic clove, minced
3 dashes hot pepper sauce

Combine all ingredients. Use cold as a marinade or hot if used as a sauce.

46% calories from fat per serving

Yield: 6 (2-tablespoon) servings
Nutrient content per serving:
Calories: 45   Fat: 2.3 g   Protein: 0.2 g   Carbohydrate: 3.4 g
Sodium: 265.1 mg   Cholesterol: 0.0 mg   Fiber: 0.3 g   Alcohol: 1.4 g

Yogurt Paprika Sauce

Served with "Whole Cauliflower" on page 153, this versatile sauce can also accompany meat or other vegetables.

1/2 cup plain nonfat yogurt
1/2 teaspoon vegetable oil
1/2 teaspoon balsamic or red wine
  vinegar
1 teaspoon paprika
1/4 teaspoon salt
1/8 teaspoon cayenne
1/8 teaspoon garlic powder

Combine all ingredients in a glass bowl. Prepare at least 30 minutes ahead for flavors to blend. Refrigerate until serving.

22% calories from fat per serving

Yield: 4 (2-tablespoon) servings

Nutrient content per serving:

Calories: 25   Fat: 0.6 g   Protein: 1.7 g   Carbohydrate: 3.2 g
Sodium: 169.4 mg   Cholesterol: 1.3 mg   Fiber: 0.1 g

Roasted Red Pepper Sauce

This a not an inexpensive sauce, but the use of prepared roasted red peppers is more economical (and so much easier) than using fresh peppers. Served with the "Leg of Lamb" on page 106, it is good with poultry or pork.

1 (7-ounce) jar roasted red peppers, drained
1 tablespoon Dijon mustard
1 tablespoon plain nonfat yogurt
1 tablespoon lemon juice
1 tablespoon fresh parsley, minced
1 garlic clove, minced
1 teaspoon sugar
1/4 teaspoon salt
pinch pepper

Combine all ingredients in a food processor or a blender and blend until smooth. Serve at room temperature.

10% calories from fat per serving

Yield: 6 (2-tablespoon) servings
Nutrient content per serving:
Calories: 19   Fat: 0.2 g   Protein: 0.4 g   Carbohydrate: 3.8 g
Sodium: 179.7 mg   Cholesterol: 0.2 mg   Fiber: 0.1 g

Plum Sauce

A basting sauce used to prepare "Ham Cutlets" on page 115, this fruity sauce also heightens the taste of chicken or other cuts of pork.

1 (1-pound) can purple plums
1 tablespoon lemon juice
1 tablespoon maple syrup
1 teaspoon Dijon mustard

* Drain plums and reserve syrup. Pit plums and combine with remaining ingredients and 5 tablespoons reserved syrup in a food processor. Puree. (Or puree small batches in a blender.) Turn into a small **microwave**-safe bowl, cover and microwave at high for 2 minutes or until mixture simmers for at least one minute.

2% calories from fat per serving

Yield: 8 (2-tablespoon) servings

Nutrient content per serving:

Calories: 46   Fat: 0.1 g   Protein: 0.3 g   Carbohydrate: 11.0 g
Sodium: 15.2 mg   Cholesterol: 0.0 mg   Fiber: 0.6 g

Alternate Method: Prepare plum mixture as * above. Turn into a small saucepan and cook over low heat, stirring, until mixture simmers for at least one minute.

Curried Clam Sauce

Substitute chicken broth for clam juice, if desired, and serve this light tasty sauce with your favorite grilled fish or meat. This sauce accompanied the "Steamed Scallops" on page 126.

1 cup bottled clam juice
2 tablespoons green onion, minced
1 tablespoon cornstarch
1 tablespoon white wine
1 teaspoon curry powder
1/4 teaspoon salt
1/8 teaspoon pepper

Place clam juice and onion in a **microwave**-safe bowl. Microwave at high for about 30 seconds or until liquid is warm. Combine cornstarch and wine in a small bowl. Whisk into clam juice mixture until blended. Add seasonings and stir. Cook at high temperature in the microwave for 3 to 4 minutes, uncovered, stirring every minute, until thickened.

1/4 cup mango chutney

Add chutney and combine.

Use 1 additional tablespoon clam juice instead of white wine, if desired.

1% calories from fat per serving

Yield: 8 (2-tablespoon) servings
Nutrient content per serving:
Calories: 25   Fat: 0.04 g   Protein: 0.1 g   Carbohydrate: 6.1 g
Sodium: 144.9 mg   Cholesterol: 0.0 mg   Fiber: 0.3 g

Alternate Method: Place juice and onion in a small saucepan and heat until warm. Remove from heat. Whisk cornstarch mixture into warm liquid, add seasonings, blend well, then return to the heat. Simmer, stirring, for 2 minutes or until thickened. Add chutney and combine.

Cucumber Sauce and Dip

Cucumbers, yogurt and dill; light and tangy, this is a versatile sauce or dip. It tops the "Beef and Pepper Pockets" on page 100, and the "Grilled Leeks" on page 188.

1 1/2 cups plain nonfat yogurt
1/2 cucumber, peeled, seeded,
  finely chopped (about 1/2 cup)
1/4 teaspoon salt
1 tablespoon lemon juice
1 garlic clove
1 teaspoon dried dill weed or
  1 tablespoon fresh dill weed,
  if available

Drain yogurt (see page 235) for at least 6 hours or overnight. Combine cucumber with salt and place in a strainer for about 10 minutes. Blend drained cucumber with yogurt, lemon juice, garlic and dill in a food processor. (Or puree small batches in a blender.) Serve chilled.

1% calories from fat per serving

Yield: 10 (2-tablespoon) servings
Nutrient content per serving:
Calories: 39   Fat: 0.03 g   Protein: 3.4 g   Carbohydrate: 6.2 g
Sodium: 145.0 mg   Cholesterol: 2.5 mg   Fiber: 0.2 g

Minted Yogurt Dressing

This fat-free marinade, used with "Pork Kebabs with Pineapple" on page 114, works equally well as a vegetable dip or a dressing for fruit salad.

**1 cup plain nonfat yogurt
1/3 cup fresh mint, minced
2 teaspoons lemon juice
2 garlic cloves, minced
1/4 teaspoon ground ginger
1/8 teaspoon salt
dash red pepper sauce**

Combine all ingredients in a glass bowl. Refrigerate until serving.

0% calories from fat per serving

Yield: 8 (2-tablespoon) servings
Nutrient content per serving:
Calories: 20   Fat: 0.0 g   Protein: 1.7 g   Carbohydrate: 3.2 g
Sodium: 61.0 mg   Cholesterol: 1.3 mg   Fiber: 0.0 g

Orange Sauce

Similar to the sauce used with the "Steamed Gingered Salmon" on page 127, this low-fat sauce provides an effective glaze for beets, carrots or sweet potatoes.

1/4 cup orange marmalade
2 1/2 tablespoons Dijon mustard
1/2 teaspoon ground ginger
1/3 cup orange juice

Combine all ingredients in a **microwave**-safe bowl. Cover and microwave for 30 seconds at high or until mixture comes to a simmer. Toss with cooked vegetables.

9% calories from fat per serving

Yield: 6 (2-tablespoon) servings
Nutrient content per serving:
Calories: 53   Fat: 0.5 g   Protein: 0.6 g   Carbohydrate: 11.5 g
Sodium: 37.6 mg   Cholesterol: 0.1 mg   Fiber: 0.8 g

Alternate Method: Spray a small saucepan with nonstick cooking spray. Combine ingredients in the saucepan and simmer for 2 minutes, stirring.

Klestene's Dressing

With only slightly more than 1 gram of fat per tablespoon, you'll find many uses for this delightful salad dressing or marinade for poultry.

1/2 cup chicken broth, defatted
1/4 cup red wine vinegar
2 tablespoons balsamic vinegar
4 teaspoons olive oil
1 tablespoon Dijon mustard
1 teaspoon dried oregano leaves
2 teaspoons sugar
1/4 teaspoon garlic powder
1 teaspoon salt
1/4 teaspoon pepper

Combine all ingredients in a jar. Cover and shake well. Or combine in a food processor or blender. Store refrigerated for up to 1 week. Shake well again immediately before using.

64% calories from fat per serving

Yield: 16 (1-tablespoon) servings
Nutrient content per serving:
Calories: 17   Fat: 1.2 g   Protein: 0.3 g   Carbohydrate: 1.2 g
Sodium: 151.7 mg   Cholesterol: 0.0 mg   Fiber: 0.0 g

Dijon Mustard Sauce

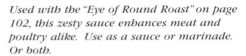

Used with the "Eye of Round Roast" on page 102, this zesty sauce enhances meat and poultry alike. Use as a sauce or marinade. Or both.

1/4 cup Dijon mustard
1/4 cup dry sherry
1/4 cup low-sodium soy sauce
1/4 cup lemon juice
1 tablespoon vegetable oil
3 garlic cloves
1 teaspoon dried thyme leaves
1 teaspoon dried oregano leaves

Whisk all ingredients in a small bowl. Serve at room temperature.

46% calories from fat per serving

Yield: 8 (2-tablespoon) servings
Nutrient content per serving:
Calories: 45   Fat: 2.3 g   Protein: 1.1 g   Carbohydrate: 3.1 g
Sodium: 345.7 mg   Cholesterol: 0.2 mg   Fiber: 0.2 g

Spicy Tomato Sauce

Don't limit the use of this effortless-to-prepare sauce. It was used in preparation of the "Eye of Round Fillets with Rice Noodles" on page 104. Toss it with pasta or use it anytime you need a flavorful tomato sauce.

1 cup onion, chopped
1 (14 1/2-ounce) can tomatoes, diced
1/2 cup beef broth, defatted
1/2 cup red wine
1 tablespoon sugar
1/4 teaspoon ground cumin
1/2 teaspoon dry mustard
1 teaspoon dried basil leaves,
** crushed**
1 teaspoon dried thyme leaves,
** crushed**
1 teaspoon salt
1/4 teaspoon pepper

Combine all ingredients in the **slow cooker**. Cover and cook on low for 8 hours.

Use reduced-sodium beef broth to lower sodium content, if desired. Use 1 cup beef broth and eliminate red wine, if desired.

5% calories from fat per serving

Yield: 6 (1/2-cup) servings
Nutrient content per serving:
Calories: 57   Fat: 0.3 g   Protein: 1.3 g   Carbohydrate: 9.1 g
Sodium: 574.0 mg   Cholesterol: 0.2 mg   Fiber: 1.2 g   Alcohol: 1.8 g

Alternate Method: Spray the bottom of a large saucepan with nonstick cooking spray. Saute onions until softened, stirring constantly. Add remaining ingredients, bring to a boil, reduce to a very low simmer, and cook, covered, for about 1 1/2 hours, stirring occasionally.

Creamy Feta Dressing

If you like feta, you'll love this dressing featured in the "Rice Salad with Tomato and Cucumber" on page 190; so good and so easy with less than 2 grams of fat per serving.

1/2 cup plain nonfat yogurt
3 tablespoons feta cheese, crumbled
1 tablespoon white wine vinegar
1/2 teaspoon salt
1/4 teaspoon red pepper flakes

Combine all ingredients in a small bowl. Chill.

Serve on salad greens or steamed vegetables.

45% calories from fat per serving

Yield: 6 (2-tablespoon) servings

Nutrient content per serving:

Calories: 34   Fat: 1.7 g   Protein: 2.3 g   Carbohydrate: 2.4 g

Sodium: 299.3 mg   Cholesterol: 7.6 mg   Fiber: 0.0 g

Spice Rub

*Rubbed and used as a marinade on
"Grilled Pork Chops", page 122, this is an
effective "fat-free" marinade (with a scant
0.2 grams of fat per serving) for just about
anything grilled.*

**1 tablespoon dried oregano leaves
1 teaspoon curry powder
1 teaspoon ground cumin
1/2 teaspoon cinnamon
1 teaspoon paprika
1 teaspoon salt
1/2 teaspoon pepper**

Combine herbs and rub on meat which
has been dried with paper towels.
Cover and refrigerate to marinate.

Nutrient content is for the rub, only.

22% calories from fat per serving

Yield: Will cover 6 medium pieces of meat

Nutrient content per serving:

Calories: 8   Fat: 0.2 g   Protein: 0.3 g   Carbohydrate: 1.3 g
Sodium: 388.8 mg   Cholesterol: 0.0 mg   Fiber: 0.6 g

Chutney Sauce

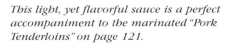

This light, yet flavorful sauce is a perfect accompaniment to the marinated "Pork Tenderloins" on page 121.

1/2 cup fat-free sour cream
1/2 cup mango chutney
1/2 teaspoon curry powder
1 tablespoon fresh chives, minced

Combine all ingredients in a small bowl. Refrigerate until serving. Serve at room temperature.

It's also useful as a fruit dip or vegetable topping.

0% calories from fat per serving

Yield: 8 (2-tablespoon) servings

Nutrient content per serving:

Calories: 56   Fat: 0.0 g   Protein: 1.0 g   Carbohydrate: 12.9 g
Sodium: 16.4 mg   Cholesterol: 0.0 mg   Fiber: 0.5 g

Seed Rub

You'll find so many uses for this almost fat-free (.2 grams per serving) tasty seasoning used with the "Herbed Pork Chops in Tomato Sauce" on page 120. Shake over vegetables, marinate meats and, our personal favorite, sprinkle on bread, preferably pita halves, which have been lightly oiled; then bake in a 350 degree oven for about 15 minutes.

1 tablespoon poppy seeds
1 tablespoon sesame seeds
3/4 teaspoon ground celery seed
3/4 teaspoon paprika
1 1/2 teaspoons seasoned salt
1 tablespoon grated Romano cheese

Combine all ingredients in a small glass jar. Shake well to combine. Store refrigerated. Shake jar again before using.

69% calories from fat per serving

Yield: 48 (1/4-teaspoon) servings
Nutrient content per serving:
Calories: 3   Fat: 0.2 g   Protein: 0.1 g   Carbohydrate: 0.1 g
Sodium: 44.7 mg   Cholesterol: 0.1 mg   Fiber: 0.1 g

Desserts

Sour Cherry Preserves

This traditional Greek "sweet" is perfect with so many foods. Use it to top cake, yogurt, ice cream or even pancakes. A spoonful followed by a glass of water was the customary Greek welcome offered to guests, and the custom is still observed by some islanders and mountain villagers in Greece. The double cooking heightens the color of the fruit and lessens crystallization.

2 (1-pound) cans red tart pitted cherries, packed in water and drained (about 4 cups)
4 cups sugar, divided

Place cherries and 2 cups sugar in **bread machine**. Set on "jam" cycle. When cycle has completed, remove container from machine, cover loosely and let it sit at room temperature for a couple of hours.

2 tablespoons brandy (optional)

Add remaining 2 cups sugar and optional brandy and return to the machine. Set on "jam" cycle. When cycle is complete, transfer preserves to a bowl and * let cool at room temperature for 8 hours or overnight. Mixture thickens as it cools. Place in glass jars and store refrigerated. (Or use sterile jars and seal according to manufacturer's directions.)

The "jam" cycle on the bread machine is a wonderful aid to any cooking which requires a 1 hour simmer. Don't limit this cycle to jellies and jams.

0% calories from fat per serving

Yield: 36 (2-tablespoon) servings
Nutrient content per serving:
Calories: 99   Fat: 0.0 g   Protein: 0.2 g   Carbohydrate: 24.6 g
Sodium: 2.1 mg   Cholesterol: 0.0 mg   Fiber: 0.2 g

Alternate Method: Combine cherries and 2 cups sugar in a saucepan. Bring to a boil, reduce to a very low simmer and cook for 45 minutes, covered, stirring frequently. Remove from heat and cool, uncovered, for at least 2 hours. Add remaining 2 cups sugar and optional brandy. Return to a very low simmer and cook covered, stirring frequently, for about 40 minutes. Mixture will be thin but will coat a spoon. Transfer to a bowl and continue as * above.

Strawberry Ice

Begin with strawberries and experiment with your favorite fruit (try kiwi or pears!) for a rainbow of "ice" desserts - virtually fat-free and definitely lowcal.

2/3 cup sugar
1/2 cup water
1 (16-ounce) package individually frozen strawberries (not frozen in syrup), thawed and pureed (or 1 pound fresh strawberries, cleaned, hulled and pureed)
2 teaspoons lemon juice

(Optional 1 1/2 tablespoons orange-flavored liqueur)

Place sugar and water in a 1-quart, **microwave**-safe bowl. Microwave for about 2 minutes or until mixture just comes to a boil. Stir. Microwave for 3 minutes more or until mixture becomes a very light syrup. (Rotate 1/2 turn halfway through cooking times if microwave does not have a carousel.) Remove from microwave and add pureed strawberries and lemon juice. Cover and chill. Freeze in **ice cream machine** according to manufacturer's instructions. If desired, add liqueur during the last couple of minutes of freezing process. * Store in an air-tight container. If not serving immediately, let ice stand at room temperature 10 to 15 minutes before serving for easier scooping.

1% calories from fat per serving

Yield: 6 (1/2-cup) servings
Nutrient content per serving:
Calories: 119   Fat: 0.1 g   Protein: 0.3 g   Carbohydrate: 29.1 g
Sodium: 2.3 mg   Cholesterol: 0.0 mg   Fiber: 1.6 g

Alternate Method: Combine sugar and water in a saucepan and boil for about 3 minutes, stirring, or until mixture becomes a very light syrup. Combine pureed strawberries, lemon juice and sugar syrup. Transfer to an 8-inch square metal pan. Cover and freeze until mixture is almost frozen, about 2 hours. Break mixture into 1-inch chunks and process half in a food processor until almost smooth. (Don't over process or mixture will melt.) Remove quickly and process other half. Add optional liqueur and return to the pan; cover and freeze until firm. Continue as * above.

Baked Stuffed Apples

The absolute easiest method to bake a delicious apple is to bake it in a heatproof oven bag. There will be no watching, basting or pan to wash.

1/4 cup sugar
1/4 cup honey
1/2 cup raisins
1/2 teaspoon cinnamon
1/2 teaspoon ground cloves
6 large Golden Delicious apples, washed, unpeeled and cored to about 1/4 inch from the apple bottom
flour
1 cup apple juice

Preheat oven to 325 degrees. Combine sugar through cloves in a small bowl and stuff the apples. (Mixture will be very thick.) Add the amount of flour to a **heatproof oven bag** according to package directions and place it in a 9x13-inch baking pan. Insert apples carefully into the oven bag and pour apple juice around the apples. Tie and vent according to package directions. Bake for about 1 hour or until apples are soft. Slit oven bag to remove apples, * place in bowls and cover with the baking juices.

Use your favorite tart apple instead of the Golden Delicious.

2% calories from fat per serving

Yield: 6 servings
Nutrient content per serving:
Calories: 231   Fat: 0.6 g   Protein: 0.7 g   Carbohydrate: 55.6 g
Sodium: 3.8 mg   Cholesterol: 0.0 mg   Fiber: 4.4 g

Alternate Method: Preheat oven to 350 degrees. Combine sugar through cloves in a small bowl and stuff the apples. Place them in a 9x13-inch baking pan. Pour apple juice around apples. Bake for about 1 hour, basting frequently with liquid, until apples are soft. Continue from * above.

Dried Fruit Delight Balls

This is a sweet treat without guilt - perfect!

1/2 cup chopped dates
1/2 cup raisins
1/2 cup dried apricots
1 cup water

Place dates, raisins, apricots and water in a **microwave**-safe bowl. Cover. Microwave at high temperature for 3 minutes. (Rotate 1/2 turn halfway through cooking time if microwave does not have a carousel.) Let stand for 2 minutes. Drain.

1/4 cup pecans, chopped

* Place fruit in a food processor with pecans and turn on and off several times until coarsely chopped. **Do not puree.** (Or chop in small batches in a blender.)

1/4 teaspoon almond extract
1/2 cup sugar

Add extract and combine. Remove mixture and form into 1-inch balls. Roll in sugar on waxed paper.

Store in an air-tight container.

13% calories from fat per ball

Yield: 24 balls
Nutrient content per ball:
Calories: 54   Fat: 0.8 g   Protein: 0.4 g   Carbohydrate: 11.2 g
Sodium: 0.8 mg   Cholesterol: 0.0 mg   Fiber: 0.7 g

Alternate Method: Place dates, raisins, apricots and water in a small saucepan. Bring to a boil, reduce heat and simmer for 5 minutes, covered. Drain. Continue as * above.

Cherry Bread Pudding

More similar to the famous French custard dessert (clafouti) than a bread pudding, this is a light, simple treat. Use your favorite pie filling.

2 egg whites
1 egg
1 1/4 cups skim milk
1/4 cup sugar
1/2 teaspoon almond extract
8 slices day-old white bread, cut into
  1-inch cubes

1 (20-ounce) can cherry pie filling

Confectioner's sugar

* Beat egg whites and egg slightly by hand in a bowl. Add milk, sugar and extract. Combine with bread cubes, cover and refrigerate at least 8 hours or overnight. (If bread is soft, place on cookie sheets and bake in a 300 degree oven for 10 to 15 minutes to toast lightly.)

Fold pie filling into bread mixture. Spray a 9x9-inch square or 10-inch round **microwave**-safe dish with non-stick cooking spray. Turn cherry mixture into the dish and microwave, uncovered, at high temperature for about 12 minutes. (Rotate dish 1/2 turn halfway through cooking time if microwave does not have a carousel.) Pudding is finished when it puffs evenly and is not moist in the center. Remove to a flat surface to cool.

** Dust with sugar and serve warm or at room temperature.

Try this pudding for breakfast. Pass the low-calorie syrup!

8% calories from fat per serving

Yield: 12 servings
Nutrient content per serving:
Calories: 136   Fat: 1.2 g   Protein: 3.6 g   Carbohydrate: 27.6 g
Sodium: 121.1 mg   Cholesterol: 18.3 mg   Fiber: 0.7 g

Alternate Method: Prepare cherry mixture as * above. Preheat oven to 350 degrees. Turn mixture into a 10-inch round pie plate or 9x9-inch square baking pan which has been sprayed with nonstick cooking spray. Bake for 30 to 35 minutes or until pudding is lightly browned and set. (A toothpick will come out clean.) Cool slightly. Complete as ** above.

Spicy Plum Sherbet

Prepare the ingredients a day or more ahead, store chilled and freeze when needed for a delightful fat-free sweet.

1 teaspoon unflavored gelatin
1/2 cup plus 2 tablespoons skim
  milk
1/2 cup sugar
2 tablespoons dry skim milk powder
1 (15-ounce) can purple plums in
  heavy syrup, pitted and pureed
  with syrup
1/8 teaspoon ginger
1/8 teaspoon ground cloves
1/8 teaspoon cinnamon

Sprinkle gelatin over milk in a 1-quart **microwave**-safe bowl. Let milk stand for 1 minute for gelatin to soften. Microwave at high temperature for about 1 minute or until gelatin is dissolved. Remove from microwave, * add sugar and milk powder and stir until dissolved. Add plums and spices and combine well. Cover and chill. Freeze in **ice cream machine** according to manufacturer's directions. * Store in an air-tight container.

1% calories from fat per serving

Yield: 4 (2/3-cup) servings
Nutrient content per serving:
Calories: 213   Fat: 0.2 g   Protein: 3.1 g   Carbohydrate: 49.7 g
Sodium: 52.4 mg   Cholesterol: 1.1 mg   Fiber: 0.0 g

Alternate Method: Sprinkle gelatin over milk in a saucepan. Let milk stand for 1 minute for gelatin to soften. Cook over low heat until gelatin is dissolved, stirring constantly. Remove from heat and add ingredients as * above. Transfer to an 8-inch square metal pan. Cover and freeze until mixture is almost frozen, about 2 hours. Break mixture into 1-inch chunks and process half of mixture in a food processor until almost smooth. (Don't over process or mixture will melt.) Remove and process other half. Return to the pan, cover and freeze until firm.

Cinnamon Custard

Prepare this high protein low-fat treat in half the time by steaming. Serve with berries for something special.

2 egg whites
1 egg
1 (14-ounce) can fat-free sweetened condensed milk (DO NOT substitute evaporated milk)
1/2 cup skim milk
1 1/2 teaspoons vanilla extract
1/4 teaspoon cinnamon

Place steamer rack in the bottom of the rice cooker container. Add water until it just reaches the top of the rack. Whisk eggs lightly, then add remaining ingredients. Transfer mixture to a **microwave**-safe bowl. Heat in the microwave, uncovered, for 30 seconds to 1 minute or until just warm. (Do not cook!) Spray a 3 1/2-cup ovenproof dish which fits in the **rice cooker** with nonstick cooking spray. Transfer milk mixture to the dish and cover with foil. Place in the rice cooker, turn on the machine and steam for about 28 minutes from the start, or * until a sharp knife inserted in the center comes out clean. Remove immediately to cool. (Dish will be very hot.)

Use 4 (6-ounce) individual custard cups, if desired. Reduce cooking time by about 5 minutes if steaming in the rice cooker. Baked in the oven, individual cups will take about 35 minutes. Serving amounts and therefore nutrition amounts will be slightly greater.

4% calories from fat per serving

Yield: 6 servings
Nutrient content per serving:

Calories: 309   Fat: 1.3 g   Protein: 11.9 g   Carbohydrate: 62.5 g

Sodium: 158.9 mg   Cholesterol: 66.1 mg   Fiber: 0.1 g

Alternate Method: Preheat oven to 325 degrees. Whisk eggs lightly, then add remaining ingredients. Transfer mixture to a saucepan and heat over medium heat for about 2 minutes or until just warm. (Do not cook!) Spray a 3 1/2-cup ovenproof dish with nonstick cooking spray. Pour milk mixture into the dish and place the dish in a baking pan large enough to hold it. Surround the dish with enough boiling water to reach about 1 inch up the sides. Bake for about 50 minutes or until edges are set and center is slightly soft. (A knife inserted in the center will not come out totally clean.) Let dish sit in the water for 10 minutes.   Remove dish from the water and cool.

Pineapple and Banana Packages

Package these in advance and throw them on the grill for an effortless sweet ending to a grilled meal.

6 (1/2-inch thick) pineapple slices (purchase fresh, cored, if possible)
3 bananas, halved and cut lengthwise
6 tablespoons brown sugar
6 teaspoons low-calorie margarine
1/4 teaspoon cinnamon

(optional 3 teaspoons lemon juice)

* Cut 6 large pieces of heavy duty aluminum foil (or double 12 pieces of regular foil). On each piece, place a slice of pineapple and top with 2 pieces of banana. Sprinkle with 1 tablespoon brown sugar and dot with 1 teaspoon margarine. Sprinkle with cinnamon. Wrap foil packages tightly, folding long edge first, then remaining edges. Place on the preheated **grill**, folded sides up, on medium high heat for about 10 minutes. Banana should be slightly cooked in a brown sugar syrup.

To prepare in advance, brush bananas with lemon juice before assembling.

12% calories from fat per serving

Yield: 6 servings
Nutrient content per serving:
Calories: 161   Fat: 2.2 g   Protein: 0.8 g   Carbohydrate: 34.5 g
Sodium: 52.1 mg   Cholesterol: 0.0 mg   Fiber: 1.4 g

Alternate Method: Prepare packages as * above. Broil packages in a preheated broiler at high temperature, folded sides up, about 5 to 6 inches from the heat for about 15 minutes or until bananas are slightly cooked in a brown sugar syrup.

Raspberry Frozen Yogurt

Make your own frozen yogurt in a jiffy. Increase (or decrease) sugar amount to suit your taste.

1 teaspoon unflavored gelatin
1/2 cup skim milk
1/2 cup sugar
1 cup plain nonfat yogurt
1 (12-ounce) package individually
  frozen raspberries (not frozen
  in syrup), thawed, pureed and
  seeded (if desired)

Sprinkle gelatin over milk in a 1-quart, **microwave**-safe bowl. Let milk stand for 1 minute for gelatin to soften. Microwave at high temperature for about 1 minute or until gelatin is dissolved. Remove from microwave, add sugar and stir until dissolved. Add yogurt and raspberries and combine well. Cover and chill. Freeze in **ice cream machine** according to manufacturer's instructions. Store in an airtight container. If not serving immediately, let stand at room temperature 10 to 15 minutes before serving for easier scooping.

2% calories from fat per serving

Yield: 6 (1/2-cup) servings
Nutrient content per serving:
Calories: 126   Fat: 0.3 g   Protein: 3.4 g   Carbohydrate: 27.7 g
Sodium: 42.3 mg   Cholesterol: 2.0 mg   Fiber: 3.9 g

Alternate Method: Unfortunately, there is no good substitute for an ice cream machine for freezing yogurt.

Almond Glazed Pears

The microwave cooks the pear perfectly and produces a lovely glaze at the same time.

4 bosc pears, ripened slightly and peeled, stem on
1 teaspoon almond extract, divided
1/4 cup granulated sugar, red color, divided

Place pears, upright, in a **microwave**-safe dish. Brush with extract. Sprinkle with sugar. Cook at high temperature, uncovered, for about 5 minutes or until sugar melts and pears are just tender. (Rotate dish 1/2 turn halfway through cooking time if microwave does not have a carousel.) Do not overcook. Rest 2 minutes.

These are attractive when used as a garnish on a holiday tray. Vary the color of the sugar according to the occasion.

6% calories from fat per serving

Yield: 4 servings
Nutrient content per serving:
Calories: 147   Fat: 1.0 g   Protein: 1.0 g   Carbohydrate: 33.5 g
Sodium: 0.1 mg   Cholesterol: 0.0 mg   Fiber: 3.7 g

Alternate Method: Place pears in a Dutch oven with 4 cups water. Bring to a boil, reduce heat, cover and simmer for 20 minutes or until pears are just tender. Remove and dry with paper towels. Brush pears with extract and sprinkle with sugar. Remove the stems or cover the stems with a tiny piece of foil to prevent burning. Spray a broiler pan with nonstick cooking spray. Place pears on the pan and broil, upright, about 7 inches from the heat for about 2 to 3 minutes or just until the sugar melts.

Blueberry Sweet Bread

*A bread machine with a "cake cycle" does both the mixing and the baking. Really! And there's only one thing to clean - the baking pan. This **is** automatic.*

2 cups flour
1/2 cup sugar
1 tablespoon baking powder
1/2 teaspoon salt
1 teaspoon cinnamon
1/2 teaspoon ginger
1/2 cup skim milk
2 egg whites, lightly beaten
2 tablespoons vegetable oil
1/2 cup plain nonfat yogurt
1 (2 1/2-ounce) jar prune
  puree (baby food containing
  no tapioca)
1 1/2 teaspoons vanilla
1 cup blueberries, frozen

Spray the baking pan of the **bread machine** with nonstick cooking spray. Place flour through vanilla in the pan in the order specified by the manufacturer. Select "cake cycle" and start. At the beep, (or after 5 minutes), add frozen blueberries. Scrape sides with a spatula to ensure batter is mixed. Allow bread to bake until a toothpick inserted in the center comes out clean. This may occur before the baking cycle is finished. Stop machine and remove the pan to avoid over baking. * Remove bread from the pan and cool on a rack before slicing.

This sweet bread is special for breakfast. Substitute other frozen berries for blueberries, if desired.

16% calories from fat per serving

Yield: 8 servings
Nutrient content per serving:
Calories: 214   Fat: 3.7 g   Protein: 5.4 g   Carbohydrate: 39.8 g
Sodium: 330.5 mg   Cholesterol: 0.9 mg   Fiber: 1.0 g

Alternate Method: Preheat oven to 350 degrees. Combine flour through ginger in a bowl. In a separate bowl, combine milk through vanilla. Add dry ingredients and mix until moistened. Fold in the blueberries. Turn into a 9x5-inch loaf pan which has been sprayed with nonstick cooking spray. Bake about 1 hour or until a toothpick inserted in the center comes out clean. Continue as * above.

Cranberry Apple Compote

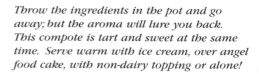

Throw the ingredients in the pot and go away; but the aroma will lure you back. This compote is tart and sweet at the same time. Serve warm with ice cream, over angel food cake, with non-dairy topping or alone!

2 cups fresh cranberries, washed
4 cups red delicious apples, peeled and cut into 1/2-inch chunks
2/3 cup raisins
2 tablespoons orange juice
1/4 cup dark rum or apple juice
1/4 cup sugar
1/4 cup brown sugar
1/2 teaspoon nutmeg

Combine all ingredients in a **slow cooker**. Cover. Cook at low setting for 4 1/2 to 5 hours or until fruit is very tender. (Note: Cranberries cooked at this very low temperature will not "pop".)

2% calories from fat per serving

Yield: 6 (2/3-cup) servings
Nutrient content per serving:
Calories: 193   Fat: 0.5 g   Protein: 0.8 g   Carbohydrate: 46.3 g
Sodium: 6.1 mg   Cholesterol: 0.0 mg   Fiber: 4.2 g

Alternate Method: Preheat oven to 350 degrees. Spray a 3-quart casserole with nonstick cooking spray. Combine all ingredients in the casserole, bring to a boil on the stovetop, reduce to a simmer and cover. Bake for 30 to 40 minutes or until fruit is very tender. Stir once or twice during cooking period.

Chewy Mint Brownies

Only 6 minutes cooking time and less than 2 grams of fat per brownie means you can enjoy these with very little effort and even less guilt.

1 (14-ounce) can fat-free sweetened condensed skim milk (do NOT substitute evaporated milk)
1/3 cup cocoa
1/2 cup semi-sweet chocolate chips
2 egg whites
1 egg
1 1/2 teaspoons vanilla extract
1/2 cup flour
1/4 cup sugar
1 teaspoon baking powder
10 starlight mint candies, crushed

Combine milk and cocoa in a **microwave**-safe bowl. Add chips. Cook, uncovered, for about 1 1/2 minutes at high temperature in the microwave or until chips are just melted. Stir. * Beat egg whites and egg slightly by hand. Add vanilla. Combine the flour, sugar and baking powder. Add the egg and dry mixture alternately to the chocolate mixture, stirring just until combined. Add crushed mint. Spray a 9x9-inch square or 10-inch round microwave-safe dish with nonstick cooking spray. Pour brownie mixture into the dish and microwave for 6 to 8 minutes or until top is set and looks dry. (Rotate 1/2 turn halfway through cooking time if microwave does not have a carousel.) Cool on a flat surface before cutting. (Brownies will continue to cook as they cool.)

Eliminate mint candies for the traditional brownie.

13% calories from fat per serving

Yield: 18 servings
Nutrient content per serving:
Calories: 136   Fat: 1.9 g   Protein: 3.3 g   Carbohydrate: 26.4 g
Sodium: 58.1 mg   Cholesterol: 14.6 mg   Fiber: 0.3 g

Alternate Method: Preheat oven to 350 degrees. Combine milk, cocoa and chips in a small saucepan and cook over low heat until chips are melted. Transfer to a bowl. Continue as * above. Turn into a 10-inch round pie plate or 9x9-inch square baking pan which has been sprayed with nonstick cooking spray. Bake for 20 to 25 minutes or until the center is set. Cool on a wire rack before cutting.

Pineapple Upside-Down Cake

An old favorite with a new approach. The heatproof oven bag, a wonderful baking aid due to its nonstick properties, produces the brown sugar topping using less margarine and therefore less fat.

3 tablespoons margarine,
  softened
1/4 cup dark brown sugar,
  packed
1/4 cup brown sugar, packed
1 (20-ounce can) and
1 (8-ounce can) sliced
  pineapple in syrup (about
  14 slices total), drained
  (reserve syrup)

2 cups flour
1 cup sugar
2 teaspoons baking powder
1/4 teaspoon salt
1 teaspoon vanilla
2 egg whites
1 egg
1/4 cup applesauce, unsweetened

* Preheat oven to 325 degrees. Spray a 10x14x2-inch baking pan with nonstick cooking spray. Cut a **heatproof oven bag** to fit in the bottom of the pan. Spread evenly with margarine. Sprinkle evenly with sugars. Place pineapple on sugar. (Cut to fit, if necessary.)

Combine dry ingredients in a large bowl. Mix vanilla, eggs, applesauce and 1/2 cup reserved pineapple syrup. Add to dry ingredients and beat just until batter is smooth. Spread evenly over pineapple in prepared pan. Bake on the middle shelf of the oven for 45 minutes or until a toothpick inserted in the center comes out clean. Cool in the pan for 10 minutes. Turn upside down on a rack to cool. Carefully remove the bag.

11% calories from fat per serving

Yield: 12 servings
Nutrient content per serving:
Calories: 284   Fat: 3.6 g   Protein: 3.6 g   Carbohydrate: 59.2 g
Sodium: 173.2 mg   Cholesterol: 17.7 mg   Fiber: 0.8 g

Alternate Method: Prepare cake as * above using 6 tablespoons of margarine instead of 3. Spread directly in the pan. Fat grams will increase to about 6 grams per serving.

Miscellaneous

Notes

Storage Uses of the Heatproof Oven Bag

*The simple **heatproof oven bag** can be useful for more than roasting or baking. Here are a few tips for other ways to utilize this versatile material.*

FREEZING MAKE-AHEAD CASSEROLES

To freeze a casserole which is **not** ordinarily cooked in a heatproof oven bag, line the casserole dish with an oven bag, then assemble recipe as usual **in** the opened oven bag. Freeze. When frozen solid, lift out the oven bag, tie and return to the freezer. At serving time, place the frozen food (in the oven bag) in the original casserole dish. Do not tie, but cover with the casserole lid and cook as recipe directs.

FREEZING FOOD COOKED IN AN OVEN BAG

After cooking the food in a heatproof oven bag and cooling, enclose with a second unvented oven bag. Tie and freeze. At serving time, remove the outer oven bag and place the frozen food in its oven bag in a microwave-safe casserole or baking pan. Thaw and reheat in the microwave or oven.

STORING LEFTOVERS

Add flour to a heatproof oven bag according to package directions, then place food (and sauce, if applicable) in the bag. Tie. Refrigerate or freeze. When ready to serve, vent the oven bag according to package directions. Place in a microwave-safe casserole or baking pan. Thaw and/or reheat in a microwave or in the oven.

FREEZING AND STORING BREAD

It's so convenient to freeze fresh bread in a heatproof oven bag. At serving time, bake while still frozen in the oven bag. Also, freeze partially baked bread in the oven bag. Then complete the baking in the oven bag when fresh bread is desired. In both cases, tie and vent according to package directions. (If your oven bag requires the use of flour, refer to the Special notes on pages 14 and 15.)

Method for Cooking Pasta in the Microwave Using the Heatproof Oven Bag

The heatproof oven bag is not used as a heatproof oven bag in this pasta-cooking technique, but as an expandable "lid" to prevent the boiling over of water which typically occurs in the microwave. Although there are some limitations, this technique has several advantages over the traditional method of cooking pasta on the stove-top: no "boiling over", so it's not necessary to stand around and watch the pot; no stirring (couldn't do it even if you wanted to); no colander to wash since the pasta is drained in the oven bag; and no pot to clean - serve the pasta in the casserole which holds the oven bag in the microwave. Disadvantages: since you can't "taste" for tenderness while cooking, timing is very important; and long pasta, such as spaghetti, sticks together since there's not enough room for movement and should not be used. Experiment with your favorite "small" pasta shapes.

1 cup elbow macaroni or small shells
4 cups water
1 teaspoon salt (optional)

Make 4 (1/4-inch) slits in the bottom of a **heatproof oven bag**. If flour is required in the oven bag, add the amount of flour according to package directions. Place oven bag in a 3-quart **microwave**-safe casserole. Add macaroni, water and optional salt. (Yes, the water will drain out of the oven bag!) Tie near the top of the oven bag. Make 8 (1/4-inch) slits near the tie. Cut oven bag if necessary so it doesn't touch the microwave. Microwave at high for about 13 minutes. (When the water starts to "move", begin timing for pasta as package directs; when pasta is tender, bag fills with bubbles and rises slightly. Rotate casserole 1/2 turn halfway through cooking time if microwave does not have a carousel.) Remove casserole with oven bag carefully to a sink. Remove bag from casserole and allow water to drain from the slits in the bottom. (Open and rinse with cold water if using pasta in a salad to stop cooking. If flour has been added, it will have congealed at the bottom - remove it.) Toss with sauce of choice.

Instructions for Manual Breadmaking

This is fun if you've got a day at home, but I'd rather dump ingredients in a machine and set a timer.

Combine dry ingredients in a large heavy bowl. (Do not include the ingredient which would be added at the beep.) Heat liquids over low heat until they are very warm (120 to 130 degrees F). Gradually add liquids to dry ingredients and beat with electric mixer for about 5 minutes. Put dough on a lightly floured board and let rest for 10 minutes. Knead for about 15 minutes or until smooth and elastic. Place in lightly greased bowl. Turn so top is greased. Cover with clean cloth. Place in a warm, draft-free spot (about 85 degrees) and let the dough rise until it is doubled in size (about 1 hour). Remove dough to a floured board again and punch it down. (Add the ingredient which would be added at the beep, now, and knead it in.) With a rolling pin, roll dough into a rectangle, about 6x9 inches. Roll up lengthwise, pinch the edges and fold them under. Place dough in a large, greased loaf pan. Cover and let rise again until doubled in size (about 1 hour). Bake in a preheated 350 degree oven for 50 to 55 minutes or until lightly browned. Remove from pan and cool on a wire rack.

Timing Chart for the Rice Cooker

 The rice cooker can be used in so many ways to make your cooking "automatic"; but timing for cookers can vary. Included are times for a **1 1/2-quart** model; but create a timing chart for **your** machine (Write on this page!). Then you'll merely fill the machine, set a timer and come back when the timer rings. Timing is from machine **start** to when either water is absorbed (rice) or grain is tender (lentils). **It may be best to turn off and / or unplug the machine at the end of the cooking time since the "warming" cycle the machine switches to can dry out foods.** Always spray the pan with non-stick cooking spray to keep foods from sticking.

DRY INGREDIENT	WATER	TIME	COOKED AMOUNT
1/2 cup long-grain white rice	1 1/4 cups	18 minutes	1 1/2 cups
1/2 cup brown rice	1 3/4 cups	28 minutes	1 1/2 cups
1 cup instant brown rice	1 1/4 cups	10 minutes	2 cups
1/2 cup wild rice	5 cups	60 minutes	1 1/2 cups
1/2 cup bulgur wheat	1 cup	10 minutes	1 1/4 cups
1/2 cup medium barley	2 cups	30 minutes	1 1/2 cups
1/2 cup brown lentils	3 cups	30 minutes	1 1/3 cups
1/2 cup red lentils	2 cups	15 minutes	1 1/4 cups

STEAMING

1 1/4 cups water (amount of water added which just reaches the bottom of the steamer plate) steams 23 minutes until it evaporates.

Yogurt Cheese

In some recipes, this is an effective substitute for cream cheese, mayonnaise and sour cream. Lower in calories and fat, it also is additive free. It's an excellent source of calcium with 203 mg per serving.

2 cups plain nonfat yogurt (_no_ gelatin added)
yogurt strainer
a container to hold strainer, strainer should _not_ touch the bottom of the container

Place yogurt in strainer. (If no yogurt strainer is available, line a standard strainer with cheesecloth.) Set the strainer in the container. Cover strainer and refrigerate until desired thickness is produced, at least 6 hours. Discard the drained liquid. The longer the yogurt is allowed to drain, the thicker it will become. Use in recipes or transfer to a covered container. Yogurt cheese should remain fresh for up to two weeks.

Draining yogurt 6 hours results in a "sour cream" consistency.

Draining yogurt 12 hours results in a "dessert topping" consistency (about 1/2 the original amount).

Draining yogurt 24-48 hours results in a "cream cheese" consistency (about 1/3 the original amount).

0% calories from fat per serving

Yield: 4 (2-ounce) servings (amount produced after draining 12 hours)
Nutrient content per serving:
Calories: 34   Fat: 0.0 g   Protein: 3.4 g   Carbohydrate: 5.4 g
Sodium: 47.3 mg   Cholesterol: 1.7 mg   Fiber: 0.0 g

Fat~Free Method to Thicken Sauce

Instead of using the old flour and butter method to thicken a sauce, use this easy method to save fat calories. It's easy, too!

1 tablespoon cornstarch
1 tablespoon wine or other liquid
1 cup liquid to be thickened, warm

Place liquid to be thickened in a **microwave**-safe bowl which holds twice as much liquid as will be thickened. Combine cornstarch and wine. Whisk into warm liquid until blended and lumps disappear. Cook at high temperature in the microwave for 3 to 4 minutes, uncovered, stirring every minute, until thickened.

Alternate Method: For each cup of liquid to be thickened, combine 1 tablespoon cornstarch and 1 tablespoon wine. Whisk cornstarch mixture into warm liquid which has been removed from the heat. When well blended, return to the heat and simmer, stirring, for 2 minutes or until thickened.

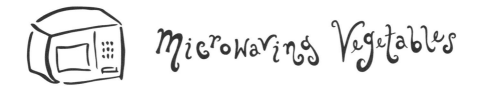

Microwaving Vegetables

The microwave may be the best appliance for cooking most fresh vegetables. Vegetables are cooked in very little water (retaining more vitamins and color), can be served in the dish in which they are cooked and the cooking times are definitely shorter than stove-top cooking. A little practice will "make perfect" and you'll never steam on the stove-top again. Refer to the manufacturer's instructions which accompanied your microwave for specific instructions.

1. Clean vegetables, cut or slice uniformly into pieces and place in a **microwave**-safe dish. Add a small amount of water (2 tablespoons per pound, in general, although some vegetables may be cooked with just the water which clings to them after washing). Cover. Plastic wrap produces a better result than the dish lid, since less steam escapes. (Don't let wrap touch the vegetables as not all wrap is food safe at high temperatures.) Make a couple of slits in the wrap to allow some steam to escape.

2. Allow 6 to 7 minutes per pound for a 650 watt microwave. (Rotate dish 1/2 turn halfway through cooking time if microwave does not have a carousel.) Check manufacturer's instructions for wattage and adjust with more or less time as directed. After cooking, let rest for 5 minutes, covered, as vegetables will continue to cook. Drain if necessary and season to taste.

3. A variety of vegetables can be cooked together if they are grouped properly. Arrange vegetables in "circles" placing the slower-cooking vegetables near the outside and the others nearer the inside. The slow-cooking vegetables are: Beets, carrots, parsnips, and winter squash. Most of the others have the same cooking times as long as they are cut into the same size pieces. Baked potatoes should be pierced to allow steam to escape, and they can be placed directly on the oven tray.

Methods and Timing for Cooking Dried Beans in the Slow Cooker

Cooked dried beans freeze well, are very reasonable, and provide an excellent nutrient source of protein, fiber, vitamins and minerals. Here are four different techniques we've used for cooking dried beans in the slow cooker. Use the one which fits your schedule and the type of recipe you're using, and create wonderful healthy bean soups. Be aware that cooking times for dried beans vary from bean to bean and can vary for the same variety of bean depending on the crop! Have fun experimenting with the many varieties on the market. An additional bean tip: soaking and draining before final cooking is said to remove the gas-producing elements in beans. Choose the method accordingly.

Method 1. Soak beans overnight in water to cover. Drain. Place beans and 4 cups liquid for each cup of dried beans (measure before soaking) in slow cooker with desired seasonings. Cook at high temperature for 5 to 6 hours or until beans are tender.

Method 2. Do not presoak beans. Place in slow cooker with about 2 1/2 cups of water for each cup of dried beans and desired seasonings. Cook at high for 2 hours, then cook at low for 18 to 20 hours or until beans are tender. Add additional hot water if necessary.

Method 3. Soak beans overnight in 2 1/2 cups water for each cup of beans. Do not drain. Add seasonings, and cook at low temperature for 8 hours or until beans are tender.

Method 4. Soak beans by cooking at low temperature in slow cooker for at least 8 hours using 3 cups liquid for each cup dried beans. Drain. Add about 1 3/4 cups liquid (for each cup dried beans) to drained beans along with seasonings, and cook at low temperature for 8 hours or until beans are tender.

Automatic Menus

Notes

Automatic Menus

What's for dinner? You don't have time to cook, but you want dinner at home? It's not impossible. Use your time-saving (and fat-reducing) appliances to create "automatic" meals. The following menus demonstrate the ways in which these appliances can be used to offer your family and/or friends healthful appetizing meals with the greatest of ease both in preparation and cleanup. **The key to success in several menus is to plan ahead; assemble and complete some foods the evening before.** Other menus can be cooked at the last minute. It is very likely that only one or two recipes from each menu may be used. Good enough. These are merely guidelines for do-ahead cooking for your own favorite recipes and foods.

Remember that nutrient values are for portions indicated. If you eat two portions, you double the caloric intake as well as other nutrients. Some menus may have a higher sodium content than you desire. Decrease salt in recipes wherever necessary to fit your guidelines.

The Holidays

A delightful meal for a special occasion, there will be no watching and basting, as well as less cleanup in the kitchen because of the heatproof oven bag. Prepare the eggplant dip, green beans, pepper sauce and cake in advance. "Automatically", the bread will bake, the compote will simmer, the lamb and potatoes will roast, and you'll enjoy your company for a change.

Roasted Eggplant Dip **
Pita Chips (purchased)
Leg of Lamb*
Red Pepper Sauce **
Green Beans with Feta and Salsa **
Roast Potatoes with Oregano
Cranberry Apple Compote
Herb Bread with Cornmeal ***
Pineapple Upside-Down Cake **

* May assemble the night before.
** May prepare ahead.
*** May set the timer in the morning.

15% calories from fat per serving

Nutrient content per serving:
Calories: 1214   Fat: 20.7 g   Protein: 52.2 g   Carbohydrate: 204.8 g
Sodium: 1693 mg   Cholesterol: 125.9 mg   Fiber: 13.2 g

Busy Day, but Everyone's Home for Dinner

Your only last-minute job will be to cook the rice, and the rice cooker will do it for you.

Pork Stew with Lentils, Raisins and Dried Apples *
Plain, White Rice
Salad Greens (purchased) with
Klestene's Dressing **
Angel Food Cake (purchased) with
Sour Cherry Preserves **

* May assemble the night before.
** May prepare ahead.

14% calories from fat per serving

Nutrient content per serving:
Calories: 675   Fat: 10.3 g   Protein: 47.5 g   Carbohydrate: 98.1 g
Sodium: 892.9 mg   Cholesterol: 88.1 mg   Fiber: 11.4 g

Busy Day and We're Eating in "Shifts"

A feel-good meal - turn on the slow cooker in the morning, assemble the bread and set the timer and later walk into your home to the most delightful aroma (and feeling) - dinner's ready!

Minestrone *
Oatmeal Bread ***
Baked Stuffed Apples **

* *May assemble the night before.*
** *May prepare ahead.*
*** *May set the timer in the morning.*

10% calories from fat per serving

Nutrient content per serving:
Calories: 661   Fat: 7.3 g   Protein: 29.5 g   Carbohydrate: 119.4 g
Sodium: 871 mg   Cholesterol: 43.4 mg   Fiber: 9.6 g

Busy Day, but My Family Loves Home~Cooking

Assemble the meatballs, puree the strawberries, combine the zucchini ingredients the evening before and you're set to go.

Greek Meatballs *
Almost Mideast Pilaf
Zucchini with Garlic and Oregano *
Strawberry Ice * or **

* May assemble the night before.
** May prepare ahead.

14% calories from fat per serving

Nutrient content per serving:
Calories: 536   Fat: 8.1 g   Protein: 37.4 g   Carbohydrate: 78.4 g
Sodium: 1092 mg   Cholesterol: 68 mg   Fiber: 4.0 g   Alcohol: 2.3 g

Gone All Day, but Company's Coming

Your guests won't suspect you haven't been slaving in the kitchen for hours with this menu. The couscous and bread pudding, thanks to the microwave, will be ready in about 20 minutes.

Braised Pork Loin Roast with Tomatoes and Mushrooms *
Couscous with Corn and Cumin
Green Beans ** with
Cucumber Sauce **
Cherry Bread Pudding *

* May assemble the night before.
** May prepare ahead.

17% calories from fat per serving

Nutrient content per serving:
Calories: 520   Fat: 9.7 g   Protein: 46.3 g   Carbohydrate: 61.9 g
Sodium: 788.9 mg   Cholesterol: 108.9 mg   Fiber: 5.5 g

Family Favorite

Be prepared to get requests for a repeat of this menu - so simple, so fast, so good.

Chicken Strips and Rice
Zucchini with Tomatoes and Onions * or **
Chewy Mint Brownies **

* May assemble the night before.
** May prepare ahead.

18% calories from fat per serving

Nutrient content per serving:
Calories: 542   Fat: 10.7 g   Protein: 54.0 g   Carbohydrate: 57.4 g
Sodium: 598.8 mg   Cholesterol: 130.6 mg   Fiber: 3.3 g

Quick Meal for Rave Reviews

Using several time-saving appliances, you can effortlessly produce a healthy tasty dinner.

Old-Fashioned Meat Loaf *
Spinach with Rice and Dill
Sliced Tomato
Rye Bread with Beer ****
Cranberry Apple Compote **

* May assemble the night before.
** May prepare ahead.
*** May set the timer in the morning.

9% calories from fat per serving

Nutrient content per serving:
Calories: 652   Fat: 6.5 g   Protein: 38.2 g   Carbohydrate: 104.5 g
Sodium: 1104 mg   Cholesterol: 72.7 mg   Fiber: 12.9 g   Alcohol: 3.2 g

Easy Sunday Dinner

A very special menu with virtually no cleanup afterwards, thanks to the heatproof oven bag.

Roast Chicken with Stuffing
Roasted Artichokes
Pumpkin Bread with Dried Cranberries ***
Dried Fruit Delight Balls **

** May prepare ahead.
*** May set the timer in the morning.

23% calories from fat per serving

Nutrient content per serving:
Calories: 786   Fat: 20.5 g   Protein: 50.5 g   Carbohydrate: 100.5 g
Sodium: 1558 mg   Cholesterol: 129.4 mg   Fiber: 4.1 g

Cold, Winter Night!

These are comfort foods to warm you on a chilly eve; without your presence, the soup will simmer and the bread will bake, and you can take the credit.

Lamb Soup with Orzo *
Curried Cauliflower and Carrots
Olive Bread ***
Cinnamon Custard * or **

* May assemble the night before.
** May prepare ahead.
*** May set the timer in the morning.

15% calories from fat per serving

Nutrient content per serving:
Calories: 682   Fat: 11 g   Protein: 31.5 g   Carbohydrate: 114.3 g
Sodium: 1066 mg   Cholesterol: 95.3 mg   Fiber: 5.7 g

30 Minutes Beginning to End

The microwave shines when used for quick cooking. Assemble the chicken packages, Mexi-corn and sherbet ahead of time and then zap (chicken packages in the microwave) and freeze (sherbet in the ice cream machine) at the last minute.

Chicken Packages with Salsa *
Mexi-corn and Black Beans *
Salad Greens (purchased) with
Yogurt Paprika Sauce **
Spicy Plum Sherbet * or **

* May assemble the night before.
** May prepare ahead.

8% calories from fat per serving

Nutrient content per serving:

Calories: 532 Fat: 5.0 g Protein: 38.6 g Carbohydrate: 83.2 g
Sodium: 874.4 mg Cholesterol: 75.3 mg Fiber: 9.1 g

Grilling is Not Just Summer Fun

You can't beat the grill for speedy cooking, especially for fish. The microwave teams with the grill to speed up cooking time for the leeks. Indoor grill appliances are splendid, whether electric or stovetop and should not be overlooked.

Grilled Flounder with Pineapple Slices
Grilled Leeks * with
Cucumber Sauce *
Red Lentils and Bulgur Salad *
Fresh Berries with
Strawberry Yogurt (Low-fat, purchased)

* May assemble the night before.
** May prepare ahead.

14% calories from fat per serving

Nutrient content per serving:
Calories: 651   Fat: 10.1 g   Protein: 47.7 g   Carbohydrate: 92.2 g
Sodium: 1261 mg   Cholesterol: 77.9 mg   Fiber: 20.8 g

30 Minutes Beginning to End and Oh~So~Good

The rice cooker is an excellent steamer and helps to create a lovely salmon dish. The microwave performs double duty for vegetable and dessert.

Steamed Gingered Salmon with Orange Sauce **
Asparagus and Potato Salad
Almond Glazed Pears **

** May prepare ahead.

19% calories from fat per serving

Nutrient content per serving:
Calories: 437   Fat: 9.1 g   Protein: 26.8 g   Carbohydrate: 61.8 g
Sodium: 474.1 mg   Cholesterol: 62.4 mg   Fiber: 5.3 g

Pasta Night

For a delightful spaghetti and meat sauce dinner, turn on the slow cooker in the morning and all that's left is to bake the garlic bread which you've already prepared and frozen. Start your ice cream machine, toss the salad and enjoy.

Meat Sauce for Pasta * or *
Spaghetti *
Salad Greens (purchased) with
Klestene's Dressing *
Herbed Garlic Bread *
Raspberry Frozen Yogurt * or *

* May assemble the night before.
** May prepare ahead.

13% calories from fat per serving

Nutrient content per serving:
Calories: 543   Fat: 7.7 g   Protein: 27.5 g   Carbohydrate: 90.9 g
Sodium: 1014 mg   Cholesterol: 32.5 mg   Fiber: 9.7 g

Soup and Salad

At times, soup and salad is the perfect dinner. This menu satisfies the taste (good) and time (too little) requirement. Do everything ahead and reheat soup and bread, if desired.

Mediterranean Pasta Salad* *
Black Bean Soup* * or *
Focaccia Bread with Onions* *
Plain Nonfat Yogurt with
Sour Cherry Preserves* *

* May assemble the night before.
** May prepare ahead.

12% calories from fat per serving

Nutrient content per serving:
Calories: 586 Fat: 8.0 g Protein: 26.1 g Carbohydrate: 102.5 g
Sodium: 1264 mg Cholesterol: 6.6 mg Fiber: 9.7 g

Summer Fun

Everything but the gazpacho ice is prepared using the grill. Whether it's gas, electric, or charcoal, the grill will be hotly used with this menu.

Gazpacho Ice*
Spicy Tuna Steaks *
Minted Grilled Red Onions
Herbed Potato Packets
Pineapple and Banana Packages *

* May assemble the night before.

21% calories from fat per serving

Nutrient content per serving:
Calories: 719   Fat: 16.7 g   Protein: 42.3 g   Carbohydrate: 99.8 g
Sodium: 1681 mg   Cholesterol: 65.7 mg   Fiber: 3.8 g

Pantry List

These are purchased items (found at your local supermarket and/or your local health food store) used in recipes in this cookbook which can be stored in the pantry, at least until opening. For "automatic cooking", keep these on hand.

"8-grain" mix
Almond extract
Angel hair pasta
Apple juice
Apples, dried
Applesauce, unsweetened
Apricots, dried
Artichoke hearts, canned
Baking powder
Barbeque sauce, jar
Barley, medium
Basil leaves, dried
Bay leaves, dried
Beans, dried, "15 bean" variety
Beef broth
Beef broth, low-sodium
Beer
Beets, julienne-cut, canned
Black beans, canned
Black beans, dried
Brandy
Bread crumbs
Bulgur wheat
Buttermilk powder
Cardamom powder
Catsup
Catsup, low-sodium
Cayenne pepper
Celery seed, ground
Cellophane noodles
Cherries, red, tart, pitted, canned
Cherry pie filling
Chick peas, canned
Chick peas, dried
Chicken bouillon cubes
Chicken broth, canned

Chicken broth, low-sodium, canned
Chili powder
Chocolate chips, semi-sweet
Cinnamon, ground
Clam juice, bottled
Cloves, ground
Cloves, whole
Cocoa
Condensed milk, fat-free, sweetened
Coriander leaves, dried
Corn chips, plain, low-fat
Cornmeal, white or yellow
Cornstarch
Couscous
Crabmeat, canned
Cranberries, dried
Cranberry sauce, whole-berry
Cumin, ground
Curry powder
Dates, chopped
Dijon mustard
Dill weed, dried
Elbow macaroni
Flour (bread, whole wheat,
    all purpose, rye)
Garlic powder
Gelatin, unflavored
Ginger, ground
Green chilies, chopped, canned
Heatproof oven bags
Honey
Hot pepper sauce
Italian dressing, fat-free
Jalapeño peppers, pickled
Jalapeño pepper jelly
Kidney beans, canned

Lemon juice
Lentils (brown, red)
Lima beans, dried
Liquid smoke flavoring
Mango chutney
Maple syrup
Mayonnaise, fat-free
Mint leaves, dried
Mint candies, "starlight"
Molasses, dark
Mustard, dry
Nonstick cooking spray
Nutmeg, ground
Oatmeal, quick
Oil (vegetable, olive)
Old Bay Seasoning
Olives, Calamata
Olives, pimento-stuffed Spanish
Olives, ripe, sliced
Onion powder
Onion soup, dry
Orange marmalade
Orange-flavored liqueur
Oregano leaves, dried
Orzo (rice-shaped) pasta,
   also called rosemarina
Paprika
Pecans, chopped
Pepper, ground (black, white)
Pineapple slices, canned
Pinto beans, dried
Plums, purple, canned
Poppy seeds
Poultry seasoning
Prunes, dried
Pumpkin, canned
Pureed prunes (baby food
   containing no tapioca), jar
Raisins, golden
Raisins
Ramen noodles, low-fat
Red pepper flakes
Red peppers, roasted, jar
Rice (white, instant, brown)
Rice noodles, crispy
Rosemary leaves, dried

Rum, dark
Saffron powder or threads
Salsa, chunky, jar
Salt
Salt, seasoned
Sesame seeds
Shell pasta, small
Sherry
Skewers, wooden
Skim milk, dry
Smoked salt flavoring
Soy sauce, low-sodium
Spaghettini pasta
Stuffing with herbs, box
Sugar, confectioner's
Sugar, colored
Sugar (white, brown, dark brown)
Tarragon leaves, dried
Thyme leaves, dried
Tomato sauce, canned
Tomato sauce, low-sodium, canned
Tomato paste, canned
Tomato paste, low-sodium, canned
Tomatoes, canned
Tomatoes, low-sodium, canned
Tomatoes, stewed, canned
Tomatoes, stewed, low-sodium, canned
Tomatoes, sun dried (not oil-packed)
Tomatoes, plum, canned
Tomatoes and green chilis, diced, canned
Tuna, water-packed, canned
Turmeric powder
Vanilla
Vegetable juice
Vegetable juice, low-sodium
Vermicelli pasta
Vermouth, dry
Vinegar (red wine, white, balsamic)
Water chestnuts, canned
White kidney beans (cannelini), canned
White twine
White beans, giant, dried
Wine (red, white)
Worcestershire sauce
Yeast, active dry

Index

Main Index

Automatic Bread Machine Index

Grill Index

Ice Cream Machine Index

Microwave Index

Rice Cooker Index

Slow Cooker Index

Order Additional Book Copies

Telephone or Fax: (314) 821-8822

On-line: AUTOCOOK@worldnet.att.net

Postal: AUTOCOOK, L.L.C.
PO Box 31263
St. Louis, MO 63131-0263

Please send _____ **cookbook(s)**   @ $19.95   _____
Sales tax: Please add 6.725% for shipments   _____
                                    to Missouri addresses
Postage and handling: Total for 1 book $4.00   _____
                                        Each additional book $2.00   _____

                                                        GRAND TOTAL   _____

Payment: ☐ Check
Make check   payable to AUTOCOOK, L.L.C.

Charge to: ☐ Visa   ☐ MasterCard
Please complete the following:
Name _____
Address _____
City_____
State _____ Zip_____ Phone (   ) _____
Account Number _____
Expiration Date _____
Name on Card _____
Signature _____

Order Additional Book Copies and/or Heatproof Oven Bags

Prices are subject to change at any time, and acceptance of each order is conditional upon product availability.

Telephone or Fax: (314) 821-8822

On-line: AUTOCOOK@worldnet.att.net

Postal: AUTOCOOK, L.L.C.
PO Box 31263
St. Louis, MO 63131-0263

Please send _____ **cookbooks(s)** @ $19.95 _____

Please send _____ **packages of heatproof oven bags** @ $1.40/pkg _____

Minimum 4 packages; each contains 5 (14x17-inch) oven bags

Sales tax: Please add 6.725% for shipments to Missouri addresses _____

Postage and handling:

Book(s) and oven bags: Total for 1 book	$4.00	_____
Each additional book	$2.00	_____
4 packages oven bags without book	$3.00	_____
(Each additional oven bag package)	add $.25	_____
GRAND TOTAL		_____

Payment: ☐ Check
Make check payable to AUTOCOOK, L.L.C.

Charge to: ☐ Visa   ☐ MasterCard
Please complete the following:
Name _____
Address _____
City _____
State _____ Zip _____ Phone ( ) _____
Account Number _____
Expiration Date _____
Name on Card _____
Signature _____

Order Additional Book Copies and/or Heatproof Oven Bags

Prices are subject to change at any time, and acceptance of each order is conditional upon product availability.

Telephone or Fax: (314) 821-8822

On-line: AUTOCOOK@worldnet.att.net

Postal: AUTOCOOK, L.L.C.
PO Box 31263
St. Louis, MO 63131-0263

Please send _____ **cookbooks(s)**   @ $19.95   _____

Please send _____ **packages of heatproof oven bags**   @ $1.40/pkg   _____

Minimum 4 packages; each contains 5 (14x17-inch) oven bags

Sales tax: Please add 6.725% for shipments to Missouri addresses   _____

Postage and handling:

Book(s) and oven bags: Total for 1 book	$4.00	_____
Each additional book	$2.00	_____
4 packages oven bags without book	$3.00	_____
(Each additional oven bag package)	add $.25	_____
GRAND TOTAL		_____

Payment: ☐ Check
Make check payable to AUTOCOOK, L.L.C.

Charge to: ☐ Visa   ☐ MasterCard
Please complete the following:
Name _____
Address _____
City _____
State _____ Zip_____ Phone (   ) _____
Account Number _____
Expiration Date _____
Name on Card _____
Signature _____